The *farmMade* Cookbook

Traditional Recipes from America's Farmers

farmMade, a nostalgia brand dedicated to preserving farm craft and traditions

Skyhorse Publishing

Skyhorse Publishing books may be purchased in bulk at special discounts
for sales promotion, corporate gifts, fund-raising, or educational
purposes. Special editions can also be created to specifications. For
details, contact the Special Sales Department, Skyhorse Publishing,
307 West 36th Street, 11th Floor, New York, NY 10018 or
info@skyhorsepublishing.com.

Skyhorse® and Skyhorse Publishing® are registered trademarks of
Skyhorse Publishing, Inc.®, a Delaware corporation.

Visit our website at www.skyhorsepublishing.com.

10 9 8 7 6 5 4 3 2 1

Library of Congress Cataloging-in-Publication Data is available on file.

Cover design by Daniel Brount
Cover photos by Shutterstock, Fawn Shear, Chris Johnson,
and Tyler Bingham

Print ISBN: 978-1-5107-6416-3
Ebook ISBN: 978-1-5107-6417-0

Printed in China

To my German grandparents Eva and Jake Feist and their North Dakota farm families, who taught me rugged independence and inspired a farm dream.

To my big brother John and sisters Debi, Laura, Jackie, and Connie, who nurtured my life past our parents' death and made me feel forever loved.

To my father- and mother-in-law Tom and Delores Long, who assisted in helping make my farm dream come true.

To my husband Rex and sweet children Salina and Robert, for believing in my farm dream with every farm chore and blessed farm dinner we share. I love you all dearly.

farmMade

EST. 2010

Contents

Who Is FarmMade?

Everyone is FarmMade! We all come from the farm; from the food that we eat, to the clothes that we wear, to the family traditions that we call our own. Each one of us is nourished by its bounty, and in many ways, live by its seasonal rhythms.

Although the farm comes in all sorts of shapes and sizes these days, from sprawling cattle ranches in Montana, to urban rooftop farms in New York City, it evokes the same nostalgia that unites everyone to its plight. One that is essential to our human survival.

We are nostalgic for the farm like never before. We've heard our parents and grandparents reminisce about growing up on a farm and wonder what it would be like to milk a cow, collect eggs from a hen house, or grow a beautiful garden for our families. Not too long ago, we were an agrarian society. We prided ourselves on turning milk into farm butter and cheese, farm-fresh eggs into baked custards, fresh picked cucumbers and cabbage into pickles and kraut, and sheared wool into cozy hats and throws for winter. Handwork skills, such as sewing a quilt, crocheting a washcloth, or embroidering a pillowcase were handed down from one generation to the next. Candle making, wine making, beer crafting, soap making, blacksmithing, basket weaving, and repurposing were all learned, time-honored traditional skills that contributed to a small farm's micro-economy and long-term success.

These traditions are still alive and thriving, placing the farm as the beating heart of every culture around the world. Through their strong covenant with the land and each other, farmers are able to preserve strong family traditions that connect us to their ancient way of life. Their independent nature breeds care and pride. These principles are infused into everything a farmer does; in this vein, superior products are made.

FarmMade aims to preserve and celebrate these skills and family farm traditions through sharing cultural recipes, farm stories, and handmade crafts that date back hundreds if not thousands of years. Everything we do at FarmMade is with deep reverence and love for farmers and all things farm. We invite you to join us on our journey of purposeful living, by farm hopping from region to region, farmer to farmer, in search of a wholesomeness that can only be found on a farm.

This book is about *all* farmers, *all* families, and the ever-important job of preserving our agrarian heritage and traditions, so let us collect eggs together, put up the harvest, and gather to celebrate all things farm.

Northwest Region

No-Pectin Blueberry Lime Jam

We, here at FarmMade, are continuously inspired by the seasonal rhythms and simple joys of farm life. Blueberry season in the Pacific Northwest is a blue-tiful time of year that always inspires us to scout out new varieties to grow ourselves or pick from local organic farms. This jam can be summer-in-a-jar if blueberries are joyfully picked and processed at the peak of freshness. We love pectin jams, but the absence of pectin in this recipe allows the jam to cook for a longer period of time and achieve a deeper flavor. This recipe also works well as a small-batch refrigerator or freezer jam and will complement any pantry or stand!

Serves: 6 half pints | Prep time: 10 minutes | Cook time: 20 minutes | Processing time: 15 minutes

Ingredients

4½ cups blueberries

5 cups sugar

1 tablespoon lime juice, plus zest to taste

1 teaspoon butter

Instructions

1. Wash the blueberries well. Place them in a large saucepan with sugar and lime juice and zest.

2. Gently bring to a simmer while stirring occasionally.

3. When the sugar has dissolved, mash the blueberries with a spoon, or potato masher if desired. You may choose to leave a few blueberries whole if preferred.

4. Increase heat, bringing the blueberries to a rolling boil. Turn heat to medium-low. The mixture should still be simmering, but slow. Set your timer for 20 minutes. Stir constantly to prevent caramelization.

5. Toward the end of 20 minutes, lift the spoon up out of the mixture to see if its coated. If not, continue to boil for a few more minutes and check again.

6. Once the jam has thickened to the right consistency and right before you

© Chris Johnson

© Chris Johnson

© Chris Johnson

are ready to take the jam off the heat, add butter. The foam on top will dissolve and give you that glossy golden shine.

© Chris Johnson

7. Let the jam cool. Ladle into warm sterilized jars, leaving ¼-inch space from the top. Use a clean sterilized knife or spatula to move the jam around a bit. This process will remove any air pockets. Wipe the rim of the jar with a clean paper towel.

8. Process for 15 minutes in a pot of boiling water or a water-bath canner.

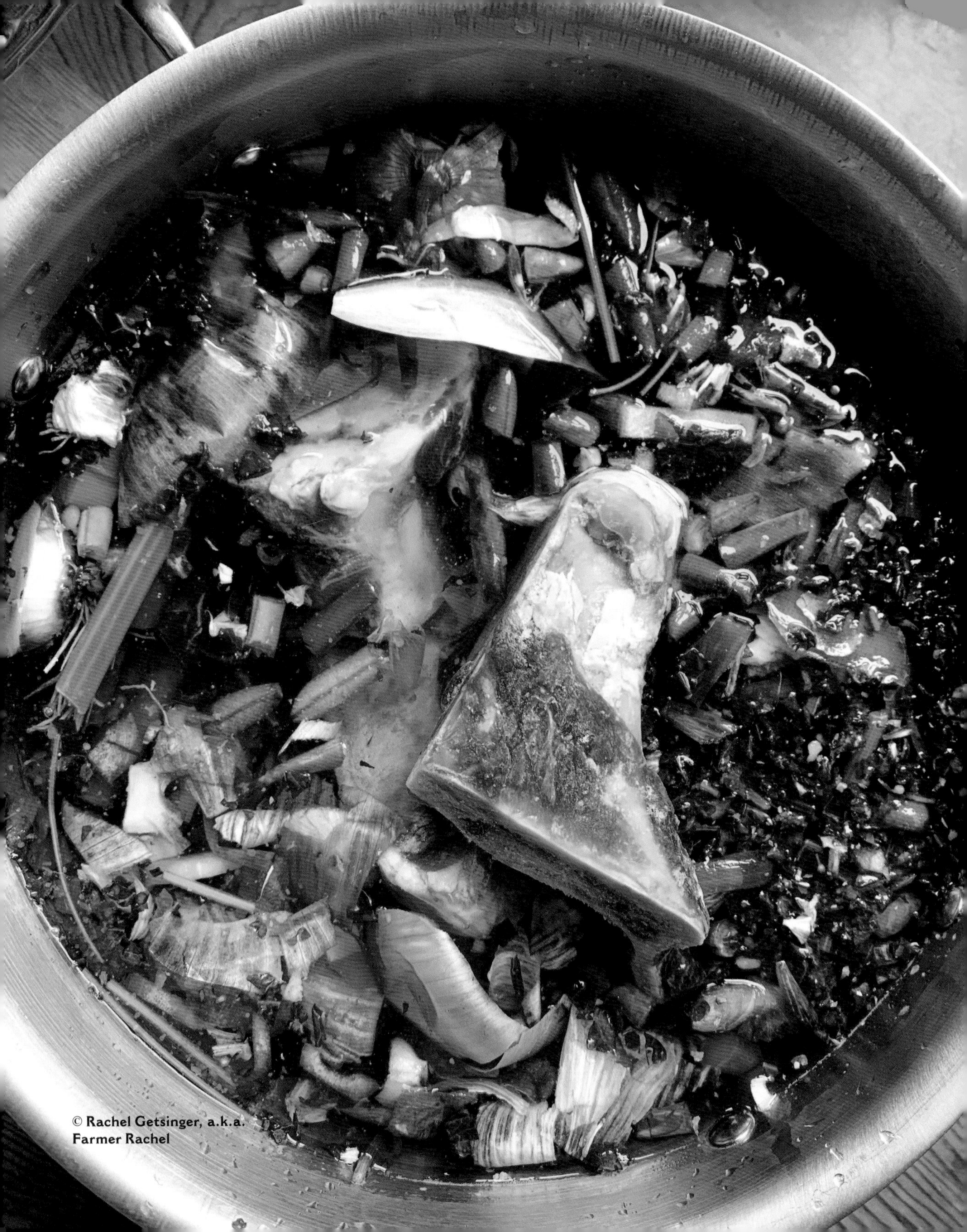

Homemade Stock

On a brisk fall or winter day, nothing smells like comfort quite like a simmering pot of stock! After fifteen years of owning Kookoolan Farms in Yamhill, Oregon, my tips for making homemade stock (read on for the best ones) have been requested most for our farm newsletters. My best advice (paraphrased from Charlie Papazian) is to just relax and don't worry.

Serves: 1 pot | Prep time: 15 minutes | Cook time: 24–48 hours

Ingredients

1–2 pounds fresh or frozen bones and leftover meat

1–2 pounds vegetables and herbs (such as 1 carrot unpeeled and roughly quartered, 1 or a few stalks of celery, 1 or 2 small onions roughly halved, and a handful of fresh parsley)

Instructions

1. Fill your largest pot about half full of water.

2. Add the bones and leftover meat, then the vegetables and herbs. Bring just to a boil, then turn down the heat to a slow simmer.

3. Sometime tonight or tomorrow, strain it, skim the fat off the top, and continue to simmer it until the reduced stock fits in a quart-sized canning jar.

Write species and date on the lid (for example, "beef stock, 9/30/21"), and put it in the refrigerator, where it will set up solid like Jell-O™.

4. To use your stock, add a spoonful to a cup or two of water to replace a can of store-bought stock. Basic stock is really that easy, so why do people think it's so complicated? Maybe because there are so many tips. My top fifteen are below.

Farmer Chrissie's Fifteen Best Tips for Making Homemade Stock

1. You just spent all day making your lovely jar of stock. This is a precious thing that should not be allowed to go bad in the refrigerator. To prevent it from ever going bad, just reboil your stock once a month and write the new date on the lid. Many, many times I have kept a jar of stock for more than six months by simply reboiling it every 3 to 4 weeks. When you are roasting meat in the oven, for example, simply take the lid off your canning jar and place it in the oven alongside your roast (ensuring it does not tip over and spill). If the stock completely liquefies and is above 140°F for more than 30 minutes, it will be pasteurized and good for another 3 to 4 weeks.

2. Never buy fresh, new, high-quality vegetables for making stock. It's a complete waste of your food budget. Instead, use a permanent marker to write "stock" on a freezer bag,

(continued on next page)

and keep the bag in your freezer. Tonight, when you're chopping onions for dinner, put the tops, bottoms, skins, and first couple of layers that you peel into the bag. When you strip the leaves off parsley, do not throw away the stems. Instead, put them in your freezer bag. Making carrot sticks for the kids' lunches? Put the carrot tops, bottoms, and peelings into your freezer bag. Sliced mushrooms for your breakfast omelet? Put the stems and trimmings in the freezer bag. Cleaning up after dinner? Put the bones from your roasts, steaks, or chicken carcass into the freezer bag. Is your freezer bag full? Perfect, time to make stock. Shake everything into the pot and add water. Put your empty freezer bag back in the freezer to reuse.

3. Homemade stock costs basically nothing to make. Did you notice? You just replaced a $50 case of canned stock with homemade stock that cost you almost nothing. The bones are free when you save them from your roasts and steaks and roast chicken carcasses, and the vegetable scraps are free because you were going to throw them away.

4. Increased depth of flavor comes from pre-roasting the bones. While this is true, please do not let this fussy extra step be the reason you're not making homemade stock. It is not necessary, but it's not hard and is great to do on a cold day when the house needs the extra heat anyway. The house will smell divine. Turn on your oven to, say, 350°F (the exact temperature really doesn't matter). Put any new, leftover, fresh, or frozen bones on a cookie sheet. Put them in the oven and roast until well-browned, maybe an hour. Then, follow the recipe above.

5. In homemade stock, the minerals come primarily from the bones (as opposed to the muscle meat, connective tissue, or vegetables). Those minerals are locked in there pretty good, which is what give you or the animal such nice, strong bones. You can help release the minerals by adding an acid, such as apple cider vinegar, mead vinegar, kombucha vinegar, malt vinegar, a beer, a glass of red or white wine, or mead. The longer you simmer the bones (up to three days), the more minerals will leach out of the bones and into your stock.

6. While I often simmer stock for three days, usually because I'm too lazy or too busy to finish it up on day one or two, I always shut off the stove when I leave the house or when we go to bed for the night. Put the lid on the pot, turn off the heat, and walk away. It will be fine for up to twenty-four hours. Really. When you get home, or get up in the morning, turn the heat on high to return it to a boil, then reduce to a simmer and continue. Another important safety step, especially if you have young children in the house: It's better to have your pot at the back of the stove, not the front. Using the front burner would make it much more likely that a young child (or anyone else) will knock it over.

7. If you are ardently working to correct a mineral deficiency in someone you love (that list should include yourself, by the way), you can smash the bone with a hammer before simmering, and again after simmering for twenty-four hours, to extract even more nutrition from the bones.

8. Collagen comes from the connective tissue (as opposed to the bones or flesh meat or vegetables). These connective tissues include tendons, ligaments, spinal discs, combs, and wattles, which is why heads, feet, hooves, backs, wings, knucklebones, and drumsticks all make

great stock. (Sorry for mixing species in my list there.) These items improve the texture and mouthfeel of stock so much that I would not even bother to make homemade stock without them. Silky, viscous broth that sets up in the refrigerator like Jell-O™? This is how you get that. My fingernails are so strong that I use them daily in lieu of a screwdriver. No kidding.

9. Don't be tempted to make a stock just from naked bones, or just from chicken feet. While the resulting broth will have lots of mineral content, it won't taste like, well, a *stock*. This is why adding a few chicken wings or a drumstick to chicken stock is a good idea. You can even add ground beef to a beef stock since ground meat is generally the least expensive option and also has the most surface area.

10. Have kids who won't eat their vegetables? Sneak the vitamins into their chicken noodle soup by making a vitamin-rich broth with extra vegetables. There was nothing sacred about the quantity of vegetables, or even which vegetables. Use your favorites and use lots more if that's consistent with your goals for making your own stock.

11. The longer you cook vegetables, the more vitamins you lose. You do not have to add the vegetables at the same time as the bones. You can wait until the second day to add vegetables. Then, to boost the vitamin content, you can simmer for two hours and remove the vegetables, then add more vegetables. Again, simmer for two hours, remove the vegetable solids, and add more vegetables. And yet a third time. Yowzah, you have just built a vitamin bomb.

12. Pour your strained stock into an ice cube tray and freeze it. Then, turn the finished "ice cubes" out into a freezer bag to prevent freezer burn. Write "chicken stock, 11/5/21" on the bag, and you can easily use these cubes one at a time. They will keep for at least a year in the freezer. A variation on this is to pour the cooled broth into freezer bags and freeze them flat. You can just as easily break off pieces of this "sheet" of stock to use in your sauces and recipes.

13. Regardless of whether you're cooking rice, quinoa, or millet, don't cook grains in plain old water. Add a few spoonsful or an ice cube of your homemade stock to the pot for a major flavor and nutrition boost.

14. Use your finished broth to make a pan sauce. Go from boring to special this easily: pan-fry a sirloin steak in some butter or olive oil. When the steak is done, remove it to a plate, and add a stock "ice cube" or large spoonful of broth from your jar of stock. Reduce to a glaze, picking up any browned bits and other juices that may already be in the pan from cooking the meat. Pour over the steak.

15. Did I mention that any chef needn't have only *one* best recipe for making stock? Add ginger, garlic, and soy sauce to make an Asian-inspired broth. Add chorizo and peppers to make a Mexican-inspired broth. Add oregano, garlic, and rosemary to make an Italian-inspired broth. No one of these are somehow "better" than the others, and each will find use in your everyday recipes! Just remember to label your stock not just with the species and the date, but also with the flavor profile. For example, your label might say "Asian beef broth, 11/4/21."

Blueberry Corn Salad

Bow Hill is my family-owned farm situated in northwest Washington state's agriculturally diverse Skagit Valley, home to some of the oldest blueberry bushes in the US. Our salad shouts "It's high summer" from the rooftops. It is made even better when you use fresh ingredients that you bought locally or, better yet, grew yourself!

Serves: 4 | Prep time: 10–20 minutes

Ingredients

2½ cups fresh corn kernels, cut off the cob

2½ cups fresh blueberries

3 tablespoons chives, chopped

2 tablespoons Champagne vinegar

6 tablespoons grapeseed oil

Salt and pepper, to taste

Instructions

1. In a salad bowl, add corn kernels, blueberries, and chives. Stir to combine.

2. In a circular motion around the salad bowl, pour in vinegar first, then the oil.

3. Lightly toss to mix flavors and ingredients.

4. Add salt and pepper and toss one final time.

5. If not serving immediately, place covered in the refrigerator. This dish is best when served cold.

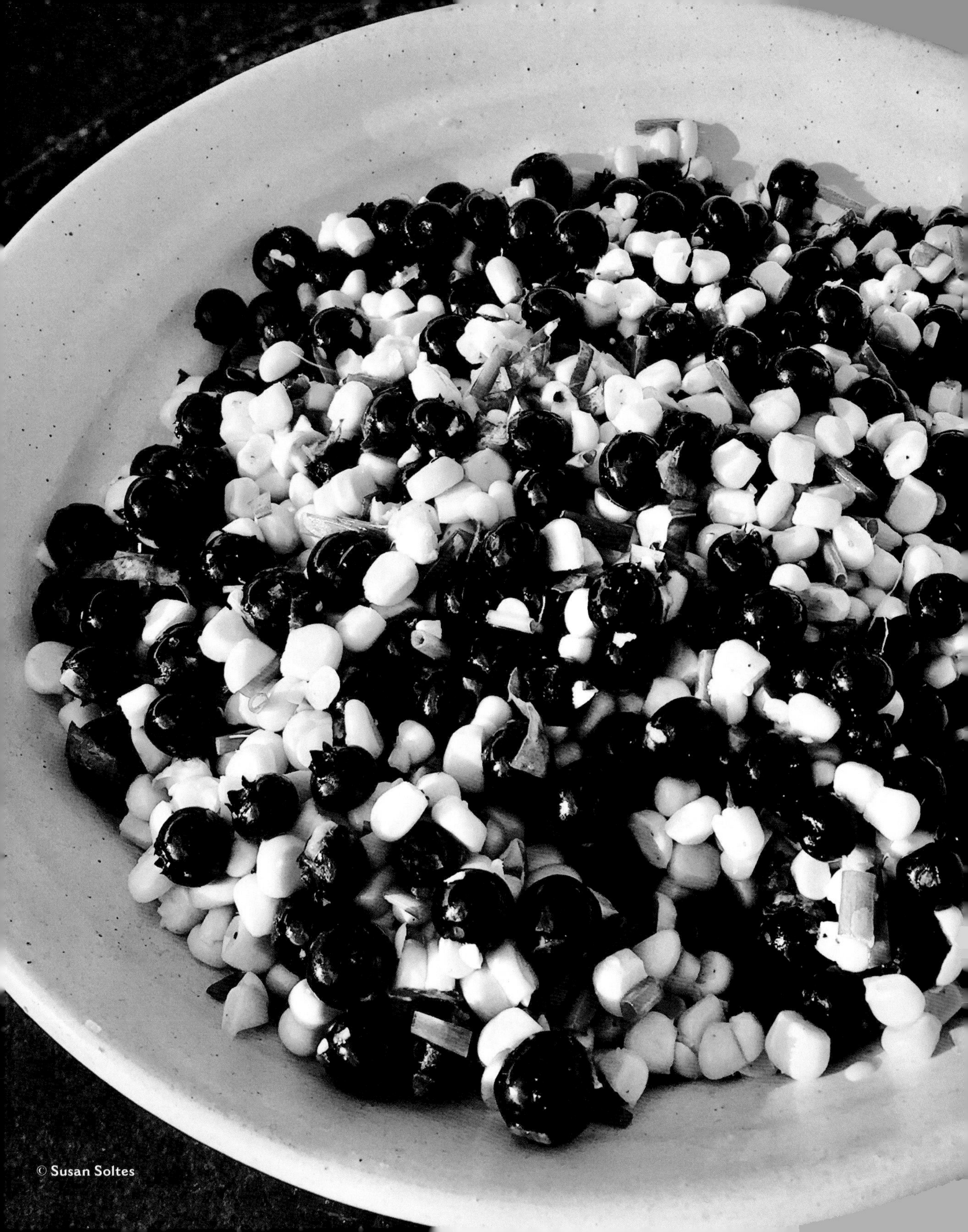

© The Duvall homestead

Chicken Tortilla Soup

Years of cooking from scratch and learning how to use real food to improve my own health and wellness drove me to start the blog The Duvall Homestead. *My husband John and I have since learned how to keep chickens, grow food in our backyard, and make homemade sourdough bread every week. My dream of an all-natural, farm-to-table homestead is coming true in new ways each day. This chicken tortilla soup is comforting and delicious all year round.*

Serves: 4 | Prep time: 10 minutes | Cook time: 45 minutes

Ingredients

1 onion, chopped

2 bell peppers, chopped

Avocado oil for drizzling

1 head garlic (about 5 cloves), minced or smashed

1½ pounds whole boneless, skinless chicken breasts, fresh or frozen

2 quarts bone broth*

2 cups frozen corn

1 cup frozen peas

1 tablespoon salt (if using store-bought bone broth, add less salt to taste)

1 teaspoon pepper

1 teaspoon cumin

1–2 drops oregano essential oil (or dried oregano)

4 tablespoons chopped cilantro (or parsley)

Juice from 1 lime

Shredded cheddar cheese, avocado, sour cream, and crushed tortilla chips, for topping

Instructions

1. Turn a pressure cooker or large stove-top pot on medium high heat and sauté the onions and peppers with avocado oil for 5 to 7 minutes.

2. Add the garlic and sauté for another 1 to 2 minutes.

*You can make homemade bone broth in two ways: with a large stove-top pot or a pressure cooker. Either way is a similar process. Add any bones you have left over from chicken, steaks, venison, or fish. You can include meat on the bones, as well as herbs and leftover veggies for flavor such as carrot heads, celery sticks, mushrooms, or (my personal favorite) lemon and cranberries. Fill your pot up with filtered water high enough to fully cover the bones. Add 2 tablespoons apple cider vinegar to help extract all the nutrients out of the bones and stir. If using a stove-top pot, partially cover and simmer on medium heat for at least 6 hours. If using a pressure cooker, do 3 rounds of 2-hour pressure cooking. The longer, the better! We use the pressure-cooking method and let it sit on warm overnight so that it is ready in the morning. When finished, allow the broth to cool for about an hour, then pour the contents through a strainer into a large mixing bowl. Store the bone broth in the fridge for up to a week, or place in freezer-safe containers for up to 4 months.

(continued on next page)

3. Add the chicken, bone broth, corn, peas, salt, pepper, cumin, oregano, and 3 tablespoons cilantro to the pot and stir to combine.

4. If using a pressure cooker, place the lid on with the sealing vent and pressure cook for 30 minutes. If using a stove-top pot, loosely place a lid on top and cook on medium heat for 30 to 45 minutes, or until your chicken reaches an internal temperature of 165°F.

5. When the soup is done, shred the chicken apart with a fork. (This is my favorite part. Watch as the chicken just falls apart!)

6. Next, add the lime juice and remaining cilantro and stir.

7. Top with shredded cheese, avocado, sour cream, and crushed tortilla chips as desired. Enjoy!

Kale-Chive Pesto

I live at 5R Farm in St. Helens, Oregon, with my husband and our flock of four dozen-ish chickens and heritage Narragansett turkeys. I am an avid gardener and enjoy preserving my garden harvest. This is one of the first garden-fresh recipes I look forward to preparing every spring. You can enjoy this pesto recipe months in advance of harvesting basil from your summer garden. This recipe is very versatile, and it can be adapted to include other fresh greens, and of course basil when it's in season. If you have leftover pesto, it freezes well.

Serves: 2 large or 4 small | Prep time: 20 minutes | Cook time: 10 minutes

Ingredients

1 (16-ounce) package pasta of your choice

3 cups roughly chopped kale, center rib removed, packed tightly

1 cup fresh chives, roughly chopped

1 cup grated Parmesan cheese, divided

3 cloves garlic, peeled

⅔ cup olive oil

1 teaspoon salt, plus more to taste

Pepper, to taste

Instructions

1. Boil a large pot of water on the stove and prepare pasta according to package directions.

2. Place kale, chives, ¾ cup Parmesan cheese, garlic, olive oil, and salt into a food processor. Blend just long enough so that all the ingredients are finely chopped and mixed together. Add additional olive oil if needed, but don't overmix. The consistency should be somewhat rough in texture but with enough liquid that it can be easily mixed with the pasta.

3. Drain the pasta and return it to the cooking pot over very low heat, just enough to keep the pasta warm.

© Stacey Benjamin

4. Pulse food processor to mix the pesto one last time before pouring the pesto into the pot containing the pasta. Stir until pasta is well coated with the pesto.

5. Serve immediately. Top individual servings with remaining Parmesan cheese. Add salt and pepper to taste.

Apple Dumplings

In America's early history, farmers and bakers made beautiful food during a time when food wasn't easy to come by. One such traditional treat was the New England Apple Dumpling. Having studied colonial history and its intimate relationship with apples, Athol Orchards celebrates and shares these traditional apple desserts with their own unique spin.

Serves: 6–8 | Prep time: 1 hour | Cook time: 20–30 minutes

Ingredients

Your favorite pie pastry dough, chilled

1 cup sugar

2 teaspoons ground cinnamon

6–8 small Cortland or other baking apple, peeled and cored

Athol Orchards Apple Cider Syrup* or other syrup of choice and vanilla bean ice cream, for topping

1 jar Athol Orchards Apple Cider Caramel** or other caramel of choice

Egg wash (2 egg whites + equal parts heavy cream or half-and-half)

*Purchase here: https://www .atholorchards.com/featured -farm-goods)

**Purchase here: https://www .atholorchards.com/featured -farm-goods)

Instructions

1. Preheat oven to 425°F. Roll out your chilled pastry dough to ¼" thickness and cut into 6-inch squares. I like to use a crimped pastry cutter for a decorative edge.

2. Blend sugar and cinnamon in a medium-sized bowl and coat your apples in this mixture.

3. Place each apple in the center of your cut pastry squares. Add a dollop (approximately 1 tablespoon) of Athol Orchards Apple Cider Caramel into the center of each apple. Try to press it down into the apple a bit.

4. Using a pastry brush, apply your egg wash around the edges of each pastry square. Bring each corner up to meet the top, carefully pressing each seam together and making sure that there is no extra space around the apple. (Pressing the pastry as close to the apple as you can will prevent the pastry from slouching during the baking process.)

5. Using a paring knife or small leaf-shaped cookie cutter, cut out some decorative leaf shapes to add to the top of each apple dumpling. Secure the pastry piece first with a little brush of egg wash, then place the decorative shapes on top.

6. Carefully place each dumpling onto a pan lined with parchment paper.

7. Using your pastry brush once again, apply the egg wash onto each dumpling and top each with a generous dusting of sugar.

8. Bake at 425°F for 10 minutes. Reduce heat to 350°F and continue baking for another 20 to 25 minutes or until pastry is golden brown. Serve warm with a drizzle of Athol Orchards Apple Cider Syrup and a scoop of vanilla bean ice cream.

© Ben Norwood

© Maggie Bright

The Neill Meal

Our family has lived in the beautiful foothills of the Cascade Mountains for over a century. We are the fourth generation to live on our small farm, and this recipe has been in our family for over one hundred years. We are two farm sisters journaling our farm stories on Instagram as @smallfarmfamily. Our Grandpa Neill (whom we call Poppy) remembers his German mother cooking this hearty wilted salad during the Great Depression. After serving in the Marine Corps, Poppy moved across the country and married the prettiest girl in town, Marlene, who would someday become our grandma (whom we call Nanny). Nanny is an excellent cook, but Poppy lays claim to this recipe. This recipe was nameless for years until one day, Poppy asked, "Now, I'm serious, what do we call this thing?" Nanny didn't miss a beat, answering, "The Neill Meal!" It's been the Neill Meal ever since. Nanny and Poppy celebrated sixty-five years of marriage in 2020, and we hope their recipe becomes a family favorite in your home for years to come.

© Maggie Bright

Serves: 6 | Prep time: 10 minutes | Cook time: 15 minutes

Ingredients

3 heads red leaf lettuce

10 medium-sized red potatoes, quartered

1 pound smoked bacon

1 pound original-style sausage links

¼ cup extra-virgin olive oil

Salt and pepper, to taste

Instructions

1. Wash, dry, and tear red leaf lettuce into a large salad bowl and set aside.

2. Boil red potatoes in water with a pinch of salt.

3. Fry smoked bacon and original-style sausage links until golden brown. Save pan drippings.

4. Once potatoes are tender, drain from water and place potatoes on the lettuce.

5. Coarsely crumble bacon over the potatoes and lettuce and add sausage links.

6. Drizzle with pan drippings, oil, salt, and pepper to taste.

7. Toss and serve warm.

© Maggie Bright

© Maggie Bright

© Maggie Bright

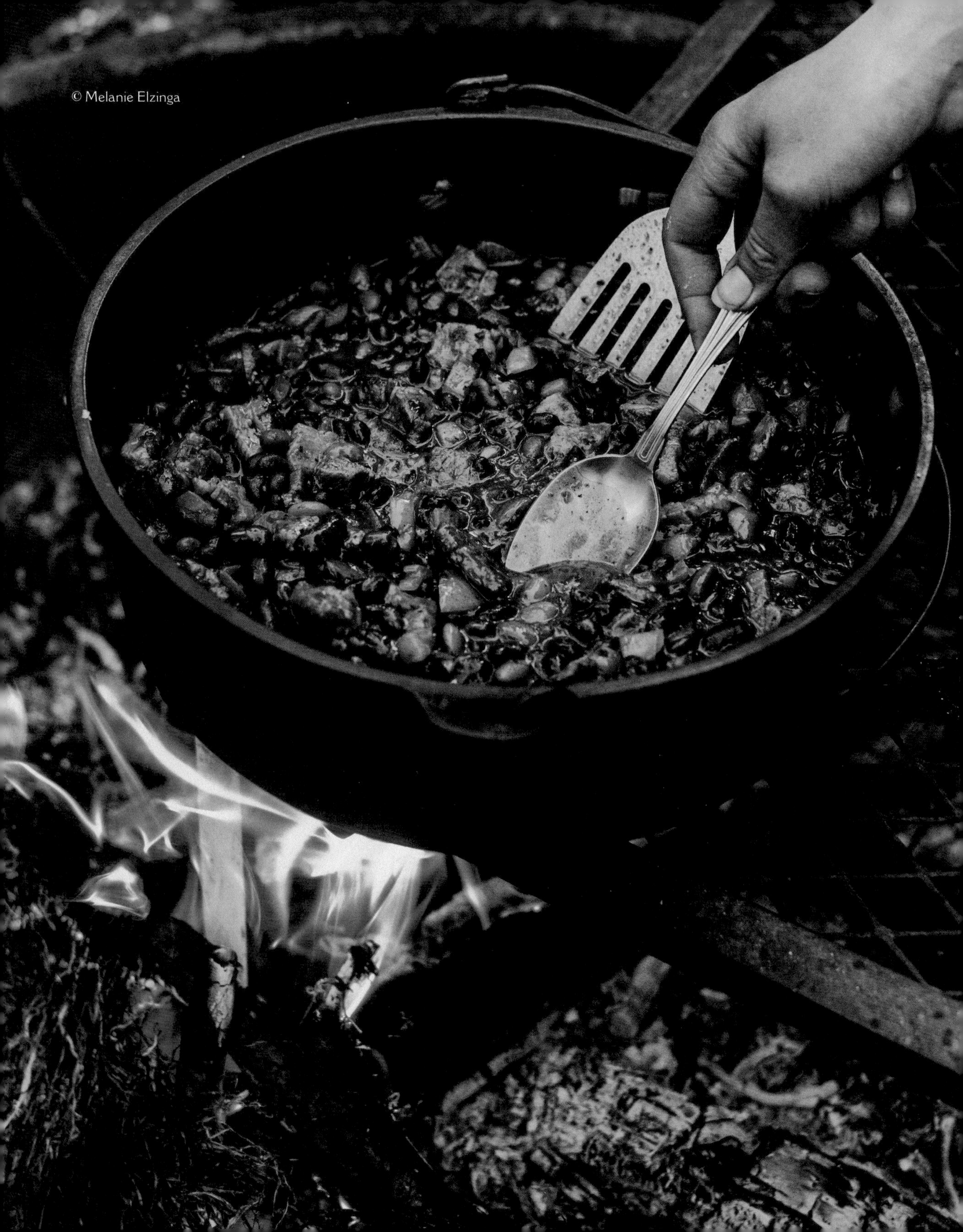

Dutch Oven Baked Beans

Alderspring Ranch is located in the remote mountains of Idaho, where our family raises grass-fed certified organic beef that we ship to customers nationwide. Due to the presence of wolves on our rangeland and our desire to reduce environmental impacts, we live with our cattle in the mountains 24–7 for the duration of each summer. Each day, we herd the cattle to good grass while avoiding sensitive ecological zones and protecting them from wolves. At night, our crew of riders stays in cow camp after unsaddling horses and bedding the herd down nearby. This recipe comes to you from our cow camp. This is fare we cook over coals and serve up under lantern light after a long day of riding. In the morning, we reheat the leftovers and serve with scrambled eggs and some good coffee. You, too, can serve up a taste of cow camp on your table. These beans can be made a day ahead of time, then cooked the rest of the way in a Dutch oven over some hot coals or in a slow cooker* if you don't want to cook over a fire. Enjoy!

Serves: 12 | Prep time: 30–45 minutes | Cook time: 1 hour

Ingredients

8 strips pasture-raised bacon

2 medium-sized onions, chopped

3 cloves garlic, minced

1 pound beef steak (sirloin tip, London broil, stew beef, skirt steak, flank, etc.)

2 teaspoons sea salt

½ teaspoon black pepper

2 (16-ounce) cans black beans

1 (16-ounce) can pinto beans

4 (16-ounce) cans kidney beans

1 medium-sized vine tomato (preferably garden-grown), chopped

½ cup blackstrap molasses

1 tablespoon honey or maple syrup

2 teaspoons rubbed sage

1–2 teaspoons chili powder or to taste

1 teaspoon cumin

½ teaspoon paprika

Instructions

1. If cooking over a campfire, light a campfire and position a grill over the top. Now, you'll want to heat up about 30 coals. Fill a charcoal chimney with coals, then place on the grill over the fire. Leave it there for about 5 minutes, until the coals start to smoke, then move so it's not directly above the fire. Allow the coals to finish heating. They're hot when they turn red and glowing.

2. Meanwhile, begin frying your bacon in a 12-inch Dutch oven, either on a propane camp stove on medium heat or placed on the grill over the fire. Once the bacon is crispy, remove it from the pan and place on a cutting board to cool, reserving the bacon grease in the pan.

3. Add the chopped onions to the pan with the bacon grease and fry, stirring occasionally, until golden brown. When almost done, add the minced garlic and fry until garlic is brown as well. Remove the

*If cooking in a slow cooker, turn to medium (about 250°F), cover, and allow to cook slow for 3 to 4 hours.

(continued on next page)

Dutch oven from heat until you're ready to add the steak. Chop up the bacon and add to the onions.

4. Remove steak from the package and sprinkle it with 1 teaspoon salt and the black pepper. Grill the steak over the fire, flipping occasionally, until medium rare. You don't have to worry about it being fully cooked because it will cook through in the beans. Chop it up after cooking and add it to the onions and bacon. This gives the finished beans a lovely smoky flavor.

5. Open the cans of beans. Drain all except one. Add the beans to the Dutch oven with the bacon, onions, and steak. Add the chopped tomato to the mix. Finally, add the molasses, honey or syrup, and remaining seasonings. Stir it all together.

6. Once the coals are good and hot and the bean mix is ready to go, dig a hole about 3 inches deep by 14 inches wide, then clear a 2-foot area around the hole of any sticks or twigs. This is important for fire safety reasons, especially in the midst of summer. If you're in a low-risk fire zone, you don't have to dig a hole.

7. Place about 15 coals in the hole, evenly spaced. Put the Dutch oven over the coals, then put the lid on. Place another 15 coals on top, evenly spaced over the lid. Allow to cook for about 15 minutes before removing the lid and checking the beans. They should be beginning to bubble. Stir with a spoon to prevent the bottom from sticking, then place the lid back on. You'll have to monitor the temperature of your coals during cooking. If they begin to cool, add more coals to both the top and bottom.

8. Continue to cook for about 45 minutes, replacing coals as needed and stirring frequently. The beans should be gently bubbling at all times. If you notice the beans getting cold, add more coals. You'll also want to remove the lid to stir every 5 or so minutes to prevent burning on the bottom.

9. Once you seem to be getting close, stop adding coals and allow the beans to slowly simmer for about 15 more minutes as the coals cool.

10. Remove entirely from the coals and serve!

Greek Yogurt and Leek Dip

Seeds and Soil Farm is located on beautiful Lazy Mountain within the Matanuska-Susitna Valley of Southcentral Alaska. Our produce, herbs, flowers, and seeds are grown in living soil within the last frontier. This versatile dip is our go-to recipe for all our farm-fresh vegetable dips, spreads, and dressings. Spread the dip into baked sweet potatoes, pour it over a fresh herb salad, or plunge raw veggies right into it.

Serves: 16 | Prep time: 15 minutes

Ingredients

½ cup Greek yogurt
½ cup cultured sour cream
½ cup half-and-half
1 tablespoon chopped leeks
1 tablespoon chopped green onions
½ teaspoon chopped parsley
½ teaspoon chopped dill
½ teaspoon onion powder
½ teaspoon garlic powder
½ teaspoon coconut aminos
¼ teaspoon celery salt
¼ teaspoon pepper

Instructions

1. Combine all ingredients in a food processor or blender.

2. Blend for 15 seconds to ensure creaminess.

3. Serve in your favorite stoneware. Store covered in the refrigerator for up to seven days.

© Jennifer T. Sharrock, Seeds and Soil Farm

Madeleines

Appletree Farm Gotlands is a small, diversified farm in the Pacific Northwest, just outside of Eugene, Oregon. We grow produce for a CSA and for our kitchen, raise a small flock of Gotland sheep for their wool, and also produce exquisite lamb. I am a first-generation French farmer in the US. Growing up on a large produce farm, I grew up finding crêpes, madeleines, or a bowl of fresh strawberries waiting for me after school. I yearn to share with my children and my community some of these family traditions. Our farm stay is a perfect canvas to turn food into art and a moment to share. This recipe for madeleines is quick and easy to make or alter (with chocolate, by melting semi-sweet chocolate with the butter; or lemon, by substituting lemon zest and/or extract for vanilla).

Serves: 12 | Prep time: 10 minutes | Cook time: 17 minutes

Ingredients

1 madeleine pan

½ cup butter, plus extra for greasing the pan

⅔ cup sugar

2 eggs

1 teaspoon vanilla

⅔ cup flour

Instructions

1. Turn on the oven to 350°F.

2. Melt the butter on the stove top.

3. Mix sugar, eggs, and vanilla. Add in flour and mix well.

4. Drizzle ½ cup butter into your batter and fold it until combined.

5. Add additional melted butter evenly to grease the madeleine pan's scallop molds.

6. Split batter evenly in scallop molds.

7. Bake 17 minutes or until tops are barely browned.

8. Take the madeleines out of the oven, let them rest for a couple of minutes, and transfer to a plate shell-side up.

9. Serve warm or cold with a warm beverage or a glass of cold milk (for dipping).

© Kelly Lion Photography

© Melinda Barnes

Sunshine Soup

I live with my family in an old Victorian farmhouse on an island in the Pacific Northwest where I write my blog Eating Buckets *and grow all my own food and flowers. Years ago, I lived in Italy for several months and fell in love with traditional Roman* zuppa di zucchine, *a silky, delicious soup made with the most basic ingredients—just broth, olive oil, zucchini, salt, and pepper. This is my variation, and every time I defrost a batch from my deep freezer it's like revisiting the harvest days of summer, so my family and I call it "sunshine soup."*

Serves: 10–15 | Prep time: 10–15 minutes | Cook time: 25–35 minutes

Ingredients
1 cup olive oil, divided
¼–½ cup butter
1 medium yellow onion, chopped
5 medium or large cloves garlic, chopped
1 medium shallot, chopped
10 cups zucchini, chopped
1 cup water or broth, plus more as needed
1 rounded teaspoon dried thyme
Freshly ground black pepper
Favorite bouillon, such as Better Than Bouillon No Chicken Base, to taste
2 cups shredded carrots
3 cups finely chopped kale, stems removed
Shaved Parmesan, grated mozzarella, toasted pine nuts, chopped rosemary, chopped tomatoes, chopped basil, bacon, or chopped roasted ham, for topping

Instructions
1. Add ½ cup olive oil and butter to a soup pot on low heat and gently sauté the onion, garlic, and shallot until soft, watching carefully to ensure the garlic doesn't overheat or burn.

2. Add zucchini to soup pot and stir thoroughly.

3. Add water or broth, thyme, and freshly ground black pepper. Cover and simmer at medium heat, stirring frequently, adding more broth or water as necessary to prevent sticking or burning. The soup will quickly become too thin if you add too much liquid at once, so drizzle in a bit at a time.

4. When zucchini is tender enough to squish easily with a spoon, use an immersion blender or a standard blender and blend until just barely smooth, leaving about a quarter of the soup still chunky.

5. Season with bouillon to taste by stirring it into the soup just small portions at a time, incorporating until you've reached desired flavor.

6. Set aside portions of base to freeze, if desired.

7. Add carrots and kale to the remaining soup and wilt until just tender.

8. Serve immediately with your favorite toppings.

Lavender Lemonade

B&B Family Farm is a lavender farm located on the Olympic Peninsula of Washington. We are home to three generations and over fourteen thousand lavender plants. Our family feels so fortunate to work together here in beautiful Sequim, Washington, and to share a love for nature, adventure, and family. With an assortment of farm-crafted lavender products, wholesale dried lavender, and two kiddos, our hearts and our days are full. We hope you love our favorite lavender recipe as much as we do. Our kids serve this lemonade every year during Lavender Weekend, helping to raise money for our annual fundraiser benefiting people in need.

Serves: 4 | Prep time: 5 minutes | Cook time: 60–90 minutes

Ingredients

5 cups water

⅔ cup agave nectar

4 tablespoons dried angustifolia lavender buds

1 cup lemon juice

2-liter container

Instructions

1. Place water, agave, and lavender buds in a covered saucepan over high heat. Once water starts to boil, reduce to low heat. Let mixture sit over low heat for 5 minutes. After 5 minutes, turn off heat and let sit covered for 1 hour.

© Zion Hilliker

2. Squeeze lemon juice over a mesh colander into your 2-liter container until you have 1 cup of lemon juice. Once your lavender/agave mixture has set for 1 hour, pour over mesh colander into lemon juice mixture to remove lavender buds.

3. Once the lemon juice and agave/lavender mixture are in your container, fill the remaining space with water or ice. Let chill and serve.

Homestead Lasagna

There is a beauty in simplicity and magic in everyday living. Our goal is to find it and create a sustainable life, producing as much as we can on our off-grid, Montana Young Homestead. We raise kids, Bernese Mountain dogs, cows, goats, chickens, and quail. We grow our own produce and are working on a beautiful greenhouse to extend our short growing season. Lasagna is a favorite in our family because much of it can be made with veggies from our garden, and there are always leftovers. This recipe has slowly developed as my family has grown, and my cooking and gardening skills have expanded. My favorite time to make lasagna is when the garden is producing, and the veggies are on our dinner plates within hours of being picked! I hope you and your family enjoy this lasagna as much as we do.

Serves: 8 | Prep time: 30 minutes | Cook time: 30 minutes

Ingredients

12–15 lasagna noodles

1 (8-ounce) package ricotta

½ cup grated Parmesan

1 egg

1 (16-ounce) package mozzarella cheese, grated

2 pounds ground turkey

2 tablespoons extra-virgin olive oil

½ large onion, diced

4 cloves garlic, chopped or crushed

1 zucchini, chopped

1 summer squash, chopped

2 (32-ounce) jars spaghetti sauce

4 teaspoons Italian seasoning

2 tablespoons soy sauce

2 teaspoons garlic salt

¼ teaspoon black pepper

¼ cup basil, loosely chopped

Instructions

1. Preheat the oven to 350°F and start a big pot of water boiling for your lasagna noodles. When the water is boiling, add the lasagna noodles to the pot and follow package directions for how long to boil.

2. While the noodles are in the pot, mix ricotta cheese with grated Parmesan and egg in a bowl.

3. For the sauce, start by browning the ground turkey in 1 tablespoon extra-virgin olive oil in a large skillet, then transfer to a separate bowl.

4. In the same skillet, add the remaining extra-virgin olive oil, then add the onion and garlic and sauté for 3 to 4 minutes.

5. Add zucchini and summer squash and sauté for 2 to 3 minutes.

6. Add browned ground turkey back into the mixture.

7. Add spaghetti sauce and season with Italian seasoning, soy sauce, garlic salt, and black pepper. Simmer for 10 minutes.

8. For layering, put a little bit of the liquid part of the sauce on the very bottom of the baking dish to prevent sticking. Then, place your first layer of lasagna noodles. (It doesn't

(continued on page 29)

matter if it's not perfect!) Add a layer of the sauce, then spread a thin layer of the ricotta cheese mixture. Sprinkle a pinch of chopped basil on top. Repeat 3 to 4 times. After the last layer, sprinkle the grated mozzarella over the top, and voila!

9. Cover with tin foil and bake for 25 minutes.

10. Remove tin foil and broil at 525°F for about 5 minutes, or until brown. Keep a close eye on it at the end so it doesn't burn.

The Ranching Brunette's Thirty-Minute No-Rise Hamburger Buns

These exceptionally easy buns are a staple on my first-generation Montana ranch. It's as easy as three ten-minute steps: 1. Prepare 2. Rest 3. Bake. You'll never go back to store-bought buns again after you try these! With a yummy pretzel bun-type texture, it's the perfect complement to any burger. For hot dog buns, simply change the shape and you're set. Best served warm. Store in the fridge for a few days or frozen up to a month.

Serves: 8 | Prep time: 20 minutes | Cook time: 10 minutes

Ingredients

1 cup warm water + 1 tablespoon, divided
2 tablespoons active dry yeast
⅓ cup avocado or extra-virgin olive oil
3 tablespoons sugar
1 large egg, beaten
1 teaspoon salt
3¼ cups all-purpose flour
1 egg yolk
Sesame seeds (optional)

Instructions

1. Preheat oven to 425°F. Add 1 cup warm water and yeast to a large mixing bowl. (For best results, use a mixer.) Add in oil and sugar, give it a gentle stir until just combined, and let it rest for 5 minutes. It should look foamy. Whisk in egg and salt on low speed until combined. Gradually add in flour until you have a soft dough. Using a dough hook, knead for 3 minutes on medium speed, or until the dough is smooth and elastic. If kneading by hand, knead on a floured surface until you get the same results. Immediately transfer onto a floured surface and roll into a ball. Then, cut the dough into eight equal pieces using a knife. Shape each piece into a bun shape and place onto a greased or lined baking sheet, evenly spaced.

2. Let rest for 10 minutes on baking sheet. Prepare egg wash topping by whisking egg yolk and remaining water together. After the 10-minute rest period, brush the buns entirely with egg wash topping, and sprinkle the tops with sesame seeds if desired.

3. Bake for 10 minutes, or until golden brown.

© Loagan Robinson

Mulberry Pie

The recipe for mulberry pie found in my Farm Journal's Country Cookbook *from 1959 properly starts "select a sunny summer day when the breezes are light." Having a mulberry tree on Prairie Home Farm and loving the sweet words used in this recipe, I was smitten. With a few changes, it was all mine. The sweet purple berries mixed with tart rhubarb is a perfect marriage for a delectable summertime pie. Pack this pie for a picnic or have it for breakfast before farm chores!*

Serves: 8 | Prep time: 45 minutes | Cook time: 45 minutes

Ingredients
2 cups mulberries
2 cups finely sliced rhubarb
1 cup sugar
¼ cup flour
Pinch salt
Pastry for a two-crust pie
2 tablespoons butter

Instructions
1. Preheat the oven to 450°F.
2. Combine mulberries and rhubarb in a medium-sized bowl.
3. In a separate bowl combine sugar, flour, and salt. Then, mix with fruit.
4. Turn mixture into a bottom pie crust and dot with butter.
5. Add and adjust top crust, cut steam vents, and flute edges. Bake for 40 to 50 minutes, or until crust is browned and you can see the juices bubble in the vents.

Southwest Region

Fermented Radishes

Jill here, with Whispering Willow Farm, based out of central Arkansas. I am a wife and mother to three beautiful girls, lots of chickens, some rabbits, a couple farm dogs, and all the plants. Growing real, sustainable food has been a long-time passion of mine. Learning to ferment foods coincided with an abundance of extra food in the summer garden. This fermented recipe is simple, easily modified, and great for your health. I want to do more than pass down a recipe to my children, I want to pass down the ability to create and give them the desire to grow food that allows endless possibilities.

Serves: 1 quart or 2 pints | Prep time: 20 minutes | Processing time: 7–14 days

Ingredients
1 bunch radishes
1 bunch fresh dill or
  2 tablespoons dried dill
1 clove fresh garlic, peeled
  and crushed
2 cups filtered water
1 tablespoon kosher salt

Instructions
1. Wash radishes and cut away the stems. Cut radishes into slices, however thick or thin you prefer.

2. In a clean jar with a fermenting lid, place fresh or dried dill and garlic in the bottom of the jar. Next, add in your sliced radishes until completely full.

3. In a small stove-top pot on low heat, combine water and salt. Heat only to dissolve the salt, do not bring to a boil. If water becomes too hot, allow to cool at room temperature before adding to radishes.

4. Pour brine into jar until radishes are completely submerged. Carefully tap jar to remove air bubbles. Next, add fermenting lid.

5. Allow radishes to sit at room temperature to ferment for 7 to 14 days.

6. When the time is up, remove fermenting lid, cover with a standard lid, and store in refrigerator. Enjoy fermented radishes for several months.

Saffron Shortbread

It's no surprise that we cook with a lot of saffron here at Peace and Plenty Farm, as we grow a lot of it! Many people think of saffron as an exotic spice, but saffron has been used for centuries in America by the Amish and Mennonite communities who, like us at the farm, flavor everything with it from chicken soup to bread. Here is a favorite recipe of mine that is very popular at our farm stand. The simplicity of this recipe allows the saffron to shine, so be sure to use high quality saffron (like ours)! This recipe is based on Shira Bocar's from the Martha Stewart Living *magazine story about our farm.*

Serves: 4–6 large pieces | Prep time: 20 minutes | Cook time: 1 hour

Ingredients

¼ teaspoon (a good pinch) saffron threads*, gently crushed

1 tablespoon white wine or water, warmed till hot

8 tablespoons unsalted butter, softened, plus small pat for greasing pan

6 tablespoons confectioners' sugar

½ teaspoon pure vanilla extract

1 cup unbleached all-purpose flour

½ teaspoon salt

1½ tablespoons granulated sugar

Instructions

1. Place saffron in a small bowl; add warmed wine or water and let stand for at least 30 minutes or overnight to draw out the full potency of the saffron.

2. Grease an 8" × 8" round pie pan with a small pat of butter.

3. In a food processor, pulse remaining butter with confectioners' sugar until light and fluffy, about 2 minutes. Add ½ teaspoon of the saffron-infused liquid and vanilla and pulse until combined, scraping down sides as needed. Add flour and salt, then pulse until just combined.

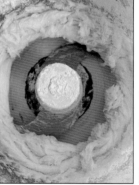

© Peace and Plenty Farm

© Peace and Plenty Farm

* Do not use pre-powdered saffron. The purity and strength of powdered saffron is questionable. Use high-quality saffron threads.

(continued on next page)

4. Pat dough evenly into the prepared pan; cover with a tea towel or wax paper and refrigerate until firm, about 20 minutes.

5. Preheat the oven to 325°F. Remove pan from the refrigerator and crimp edges with a fork. Cut into 4 to 6 wedges with a sharp knife, being careful not to damage the edges. Poke all over with a skewer or fork. Doing this allows for even cooking and for moisture to be released.

6. Brush remaining saffron-infused wine over top with a pastry brush; sprinkle generously with granulated sugar (using a fine-mesh strainer works great for this).

7. Bake until firm and golden around edges, 30 to 35 minutes. Let cool slightly in the pan on a wire rack, then re-slice the wedges with a serrated knife, remove pieces and let cool completely on the rack.

8. Shortbread can be stored in an airtight container at room temperature for up to 1 week.

© Peace and Plenty Farm

© Peace and Plenty Farm

Chèvre with Marinated Peaches and Heirloom Tomatoes

Through faith, our family moved from California to open the only Arkansas goat dairy and cow creamery. We began building White River Creamery and growing our herd in 2011. We now have over 100 ADGA registered Nigerian Dwarf goats on fifteen acres of pasture in Elkins, Arkansas. We make a variety of cheeses: chèvre, fromage blanc, feta, ricotta, Caillou Noir, halloumi, cheddar, and our southern favorite pimento cheese. We love being able to use fresh produce in this quick, no-bake appetizer.

Serves: 4–6 | Prep time: 20 minutes

Ingredients

1 heirloom tomato, cored and cut into 1-inch pieces

2 peaches, cored and cut into 1-inch pieces

Thinly sliced basil, to taste

Finely chopped chives, to taste

Extra-virgin olive oil, to taste

Juice of ¼ lemon

Sea salt, to taste

5 ounces Chèvre or fromage blanc

Cracked black pepper, to taste

Instructions

1. Place tomatoes, peaches, basil, and chives into a bowl and drizzle with olive oil, lemon juice, and sea salt. Toss gently. Taste and adjust herbs and salt as needed.

2. On a large plate, spread the cheese out, making sure to create a pocket for the marinated fruit. Gently pour the fruit onto the cheese and garnish with cracked black pepper. Serve immediately.

© White River Creamery

© Renee Woods

Mountain Woods Farm's Chicken Cacciatore

Mountain Woods Farm is a first-generation female-run farm nestled in the foothills of the Rocky Mountains at just under ten thousand feet in beautiful Colorado. The home of Highland Cattle, Nigerian Dwarf Goats, Jacob Sheep, Kunekune Pigs, and various poultry (chickens, ducks, turkeys, and peafowl), at Mountain Woods Farm you'll also find a working team of incredible livestock guardian dogs (LGDs) who work 24–7 to keep their charges safe from predators. They are the single most important part of the farm! We are all about quick meals, comfort food, and flavor up in the farmhouse. My chicken cacciatore is a classic one! It's simple to make, super delicious, and can be reheated.

Serves: 4 | Prep time: 10 minutes | Cook time: 60 minutes

Ingredients

3 tablespoons unsalted butter

⅓ cup olive oil

4 chicken breasts

½ tablespoon salt, plus more to taste

½ tablespoon pepper, plus more to taste

½ tablespoon ground thyme, plus more to taste

½ tablespoon garlic powder, plus more to taste

1 cup all-purpose flour

4 bell peppers (any color), cored and sliced

½ tablespoon onion powder

¼ tablespoon turmeric

1 cup low-sodium chicken broth

1 (28-ounce) can diced tomatoes

1 pound pasta (I use egg noodles)

Instructions

1. Preheat your oven to 350°F.

2. Heat butter and olive oil in a skillet on medium-high heat.

3. Season chicken breasts to taste with salt, pepper, ground thyme, and garlic powder. Dredge your chicken breasts in flour and place them in your skillet to brown both sides, about 2 to 3 minutes on each side.

4. Remove chicken breasts from skillet and place on a clean plate.

5. Add bell peppers to the same skillet and sauté for about 2 minutes. Add the rest of your seasonings to the skillet and stir until peppers become soft. Add chicken broth to the skillet and allow it to bubble. Pour in diced tomatoes and stir well.

6. Add chicken back to the skillet and spoon some of the peppers, tomatoes, and juices on top of each breast.

7. Cover your skillet and place in the oven for 45 minutes.

8. After 45 minutes, remove the lid, increase the oven temperature to 375°F, and cook for an additional 15 minutes.

9. While that is cooking, bring a pot of water to a boil and cook your pasta according to package directions.

10. Plate your pasta, spoon your peppers, tomatoes, and juices over your pasta. Serve with a chicken breast (or two!) and spoon any extra juices on top. Enjoy!

Blue Ribbon Banana Bread

I am a fourth-generation ranch-her who currently lives in the mountains of Northern New Mexico and chronicles her farm life as @newmexicoranchwife on Instagram. My husband and I manage a large cattle/guest ranch with the "help" of our three small children. Whether it's kids, branding crews, or elite guests, shoving food into people's mouths is one of my favorite parts of ranch living. I believe that regardless of the dish, when it's served with a good heart (and lots of butter) you can win over any crowd! When we lived in Northern California, my husband managed a large cattle grazing operation and I was the ranch chef. Six days a week I would prepare a community meal for no less than five hungry ranch hands. I relied on quick, foolproof, and delicious recipes! This banana bread was a fan favorite for cowboys and kiddos alike, and even won Best of Show at the county fair. Slather it with butter for breakfast or serve it for dessert—it will never disappoint!

Serves: 1 loaf | Prep time: 15 minutes | Cook time: 50–60 minutes

Ingredients

2–3 ripe bananas, peeled (Pro tip: The riper your bananas are, the more banana flavor your bread will have!)

⅓ cup melted butter, salted or unsalted

1 teaspoon baking soda

Pinch salt

1 cup sugar (or ½ cup if you would like it less sweet)

1 large egg, beaten

1 teaspoon vanilla extract

1½ cups all-purpose flour

Instructions

1. Preheat your oven to 350°F and grease a loaf pan.

2. In a mixing bowl, mash the ripe bananas with a fork until completely smooth. If you have an electric mixer, you can mix on medium speed. Mix the melted butter into the mashed bananas.

3. Mix in the baking soda and salt followed by the sugar, egg, and vanilla. Mix in the flour gradually.

4. Pour the batter into your greased loaf pan. Bake for approximately 50 to 60 minutes at 350°F.

5. Remove from the oven and let your bread sit in the pan for several minutes. Once cooled, remove the banana bread from the pan, and slice. Enjoy!

© Amanda Cox

Ranch Eggs

I live on and run a ranch in Southwest Texas that has been in my family for generations. We have been in continuous operation as a sheep and goat ranch for over one hundred years. It has been a blessing to raise my children here, where heritage runs deep. You can follow my Texas ranch journey on Instagram as @lonestarbarn. Huevos Rancheros or "Ranch Eggs" are a favorite down here on the Texas–Mexico border. A traditional Mexican stick-to-your-ribs breakfast, sunny-side up fried eggs with corn tortillas, refried beans, and a traditional ranchero sauce will have you begging for "mas!"

Serves: 6 | Prep time: 10 minutes | Cook time: 40 minutes

Ingredients

2 tablespoons extra-virgin olive oil
½ large white onion, chopped
3 Roma tomatoes, diced, or 1 (14-ounce) can diced tomatoes with juice
1–2 fresh jalapeños, chopped (remove seeds for less heat)
3 cloves garlic, minced
1–2 cans chipotle peppers in adobo sauce
¼ cup cilantro, chopped
1 teaspoon dried oregano
1 teaspoon dried cumin
¼ teaspoon salt
½ cup chicken broth
1 (14-ounce) can refried beans (or homemade refried beans)
Juice from 1 lime
2 tablespoons butter
6 corn tortillas
6 eggs
Choice of cheese, for topping (Mexican Cotija cheese is authentic)
1 avocado, pitted and sliced (optional)

Instructions

1. Heat olive oil in a skillet. Sauté onion, tomatoes, and jalapeño(s) for 5 minutes.

2. Add garlic, chipotle peppers, cilantro, and spices. Sauté for 5 more minutes.

3. Add chicken broth, turn heat to low, and simmer for 30 minutes. This is where the magic happens.

4. While ranchero sauce is simmering, warm refried beans in a saucepan or in the microwave.

5. In a blender, blend ranchero sauce with lime juice to desired consistency (chunky or smooth).

6. To a clean skillet, add 2 tablespoons butter. Soften corn tortillas, one at a time, in butter until soft and beginning to get brown spots. Remove tortillas to plates or platter.

7. In the same skillet, fry eggs sunny-side up (add more butter if necessary).

8. Spread each tortilla with a layer of warm refried beans, top with a fried egg, and spoon ranchero sauce over the top. Garnish with a sprinkle of your cheese of choice and sliced avocado, if desired.

© Shawn Creamer

Red Beef Enchiladas

Like the generations of strong men and women before us, ranching is our heritage. We are thankful to continue to raise beef to feed families, appreciating the land and livestock that fill our days from sunup to sundown. I share these precious ranch stories on Instagram as @texasranchmama. Living near our southern neighbors in Far West Texas, you can be sure that Mexican cuisine is a favorite. Red Beef Enchiladas is the perfect recipe for when you are craving some delicious Mexican food, or you need to feed a crew of hardworking folks. In a baking dish in the oven or in a Dutch oven over the campfire, the way you cook this dish is up to you!

Serves: 10 | Prep time: 30 minutes | Cook time: 15–25 minutes

Ingredients

⅓ cup extra-virgin olive oil

¾ cup flour

3–4 tablespoons chili powder (for less spice, add less chili)

6 cups beef broth

½ (6-ounce) can tomato paste

1 teaspoon salt

1 teaspoon onion powder

2 teaspoons garlic powder

1 teaspoon cumin

2 pounds cooked ground beef

28–30 corn tortillas

3 cups shredded cheddar cheese

Instructions

1. Preheat oven to 350°F. Add olive oil to a saucepan over medium heat.

2. In a separate bowl combine the flour and chili powder and whisk this mixture into the saucepan with the olive oil. Brown for about 2 minutes.

3. Slowly add in the beef broth, whisking as you pour. Add tomato paste and whisk well. Then, whisk in salt, onion powder, garlic powder, and cumin.

4. Pour about ¼ to ⅔ cup of enchilada sauce into the bottom of a baking dish or Dutch oven. Add a layer of ground beef on top, add corn tortillas on top of that, and sprinkle a layer of cheese on top. Continue layering the ground beef, corn tortillas, and cheese. Pour remaining enchilada sauce and sprinkle remaining cheese on top.

5. Bake in the oven for 25 minutes or Dutch oven for 15 to 20 minutes.

© Rachel Mellard

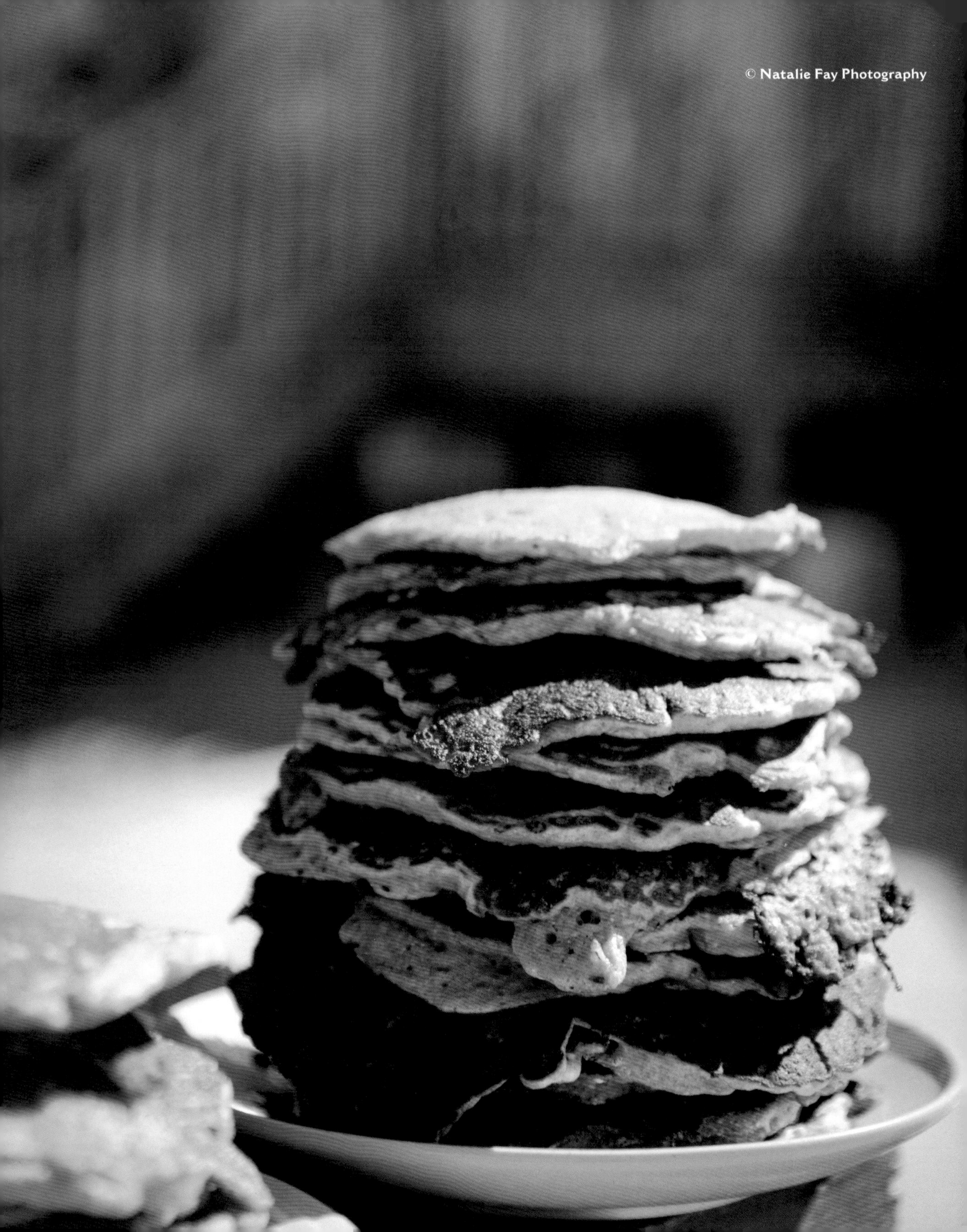

Utah Farm Girl Flapjacks

Red Acre Farm CSA is a year-round, biodynamic farm in Cedar City, Utah. We love visitors and welcome the public to our many events, always focusing on the food we grow and raise or food from nearby farms and ranches. These flapjacks with homemade Apricot Vanilla Bean Jam have become a favorite here on the farm, served to hundreds of people on the last Saturday of the month at our "Breakfast on the Farm." The secret to these flapjacks is the butter.

Serves: 8 | Prep time: 15 minutes | Cook time: 10 minutes

Ingredients
1½ cups whole wheat flour
1 cup all-purpose flour
1 cup oats
½ cup cornmeal
1 tablespoon aluminum-
    free baking powder
2 teaspoons baking soda
1 teaspoon salt
1½ sticks cold butter
4 cups buttermilk or milk
4 eggs
½ cup honey
¾ cup chopped pecans
    (optional)

Instructions
1. Combine whole wheat flour, all-purpose flour, oats, cornmeal, baking powder, baking soda, and salt in a food processor and pulse for 1 or 2 minutes until well blended.*

2. Cut your cold butter into ¼-inch chunks.

3. In a large mixing bowl, combine your dry ingredients with butter, milk, and eggs. Mix well.

4. Add in honey and pecans if desired.

5. Heat a cast-iron griddle or skillet and brush with butter. You will only need to butter your pan once.

6. Ladle your batter onto the skillet. The butter in the batter will melt and make beautiful pockets in your pancakes. Cook until golden on both sides. Serve with a jar of farm preserves and more butter!

*The dry ingredients can be mixed ahead of time and stored for up to 4 months. We always have a jar of this flapjack mix on our counter in the farmhouse.

Green Chili Queso Blanco

Our family farm, Enchanted Land and Cattle, is located in beautiful New Mexico. In the Southwest, our food is known for having lots of spice and flavor. Growing up in New Mexico means that there is usually a little (or a lot) of green chile in everything. We take our green chile pretty seriously. And, as a dairy farmer, I think the best thing to pair with green chile is cheese. This Queso Blanco is actually my dad's recipe and it was inspired by the queso at one of our favorite Mexican restaurants. It is spicy, creamy, and so good. I hope y'all enjoy this recipe as much as we do!

Serves: 8 | Prep time: 30 minutes | Cook time: 30 minutes

Ingredients

6 ounces fresh or frozen green chiles, chopped

6 ounces pepper jack cheese, shredded

12 ounces cream cheese

6 ounces hot sausage, cooked and drained

1 cup heavy whipping cream

Instructions

1. Combine all ingredients in a small crockpot. If using frozen green chile, make sure it is defrosted and drained. Crumble sausage into small pieces.

2. Heat on high, stirring frequently, until all the cheese is melted, and ingredients are well mixed.

3. Serve immediately with tortilla chips or make ahead to serve later. If making ahead, store in an airtight container in the refrigerator. If you are making this recipe for a larger crowd, double the recipe and use a standard size crockpot.

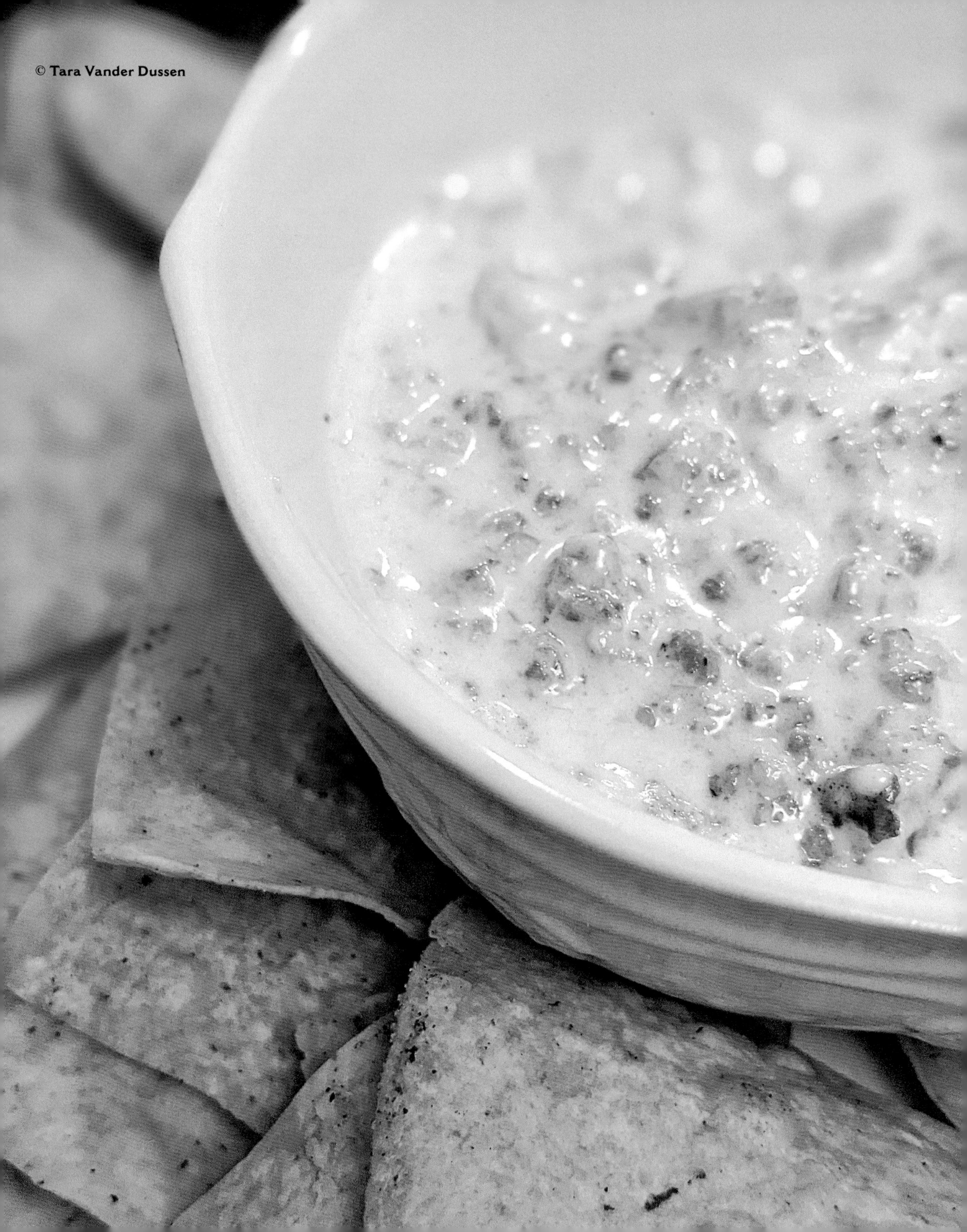

Five Heart Farms's Chili

Five Heart Farms was born in 2017 and sharing our homegrown meats with families across the country has been a dream come true for us. This recipe is one that took us a while to master. This chili is not only delicious, but one that family and friends have ranted and raved over. If you're looking to wow your family with a chili recipe that just feels a little more special, this will be your next famous chili recipe!

Serves: 6–8 | Prep time: 10 minutes | Cook time: 30 minutes

Ingredients

2 pounds dry-aged ground beef
4 tablespoons extra-virgin olive oil
1 yellow onion, chopped
1 green bell pepper, chopped
4 cloves garlic, minced
¼ cup flat-leaf Italian parsley, finely chopped
2 jalapeños, finely chopped (optional)
3 tablespoons chili powder
2 teaspoons cumin
1 teaspoon sugar
1 teaspoon oregano
1 teaspoon salt
1 teaspoon pepper
¼ teaspoon cayenne pepper
1 small can diced green chiles
5¾ cups (46 ounces) tomato juice
2 (15-ounce) cans diced tomatoes
1 (15-ounce) can tomato sauce
1 (15-ounce) can kidney beans, drained and rinsed
1 (15-ounce) can pinto beans, drained and rinsed
Shredded cheese and sour cream, for topping

Instructions

1. In a large skillet, cook ground beef over medium-high heat until it is no longer pink. Transfer to a bowl. Drain excess grease from skillet, but do not clean.

2. Add olive oil to the skillet. Add the onion, bell pepper, garlic, parsley, and jalapeños (if using) and cook over medium heat, stirring occasionally, until onions are soft and fragrant, about 5 minutes. Remove from heat and add the chili powder, cumin, sugar, oregano, salt, pepper, and cayenne. Stir until combined.

3. Add your meat-veggie mixture and all other ingredients to a slow cooker or Instant Pot. In a slow cooker, cook on low for 7 to 8 hours. In an Instant Pot, cook for 30 minutes. Serve warm with shredded cheese and sour cream on top.

Homemade White Bread

Making bread from scratch is like sharing a piece of my heart. When my sons were young, knowing I was providing healthy, homemade foods for our meals was important. My belief in healthy foods has grown into a passion at Trail of Faith Ranch, where we raise solely grass-fed beef from our Texas Longhorn Cattle, along with pastured broilers, and a variety of beautifully colored eggs from our laying hens. We have recently opened "The Market" here on our ranch to offer healthy, fresh foods (and, yes, this bread is a popular item, along with my homemade jam!).

Serves: 2 loaves | Prep time: 20 minutes | Rising time: 45 minutes | Cook time: 40 minutes

Ingredients

1 tablespoon or 1 package active dry yeast

1 cup warm water (at less than 150°F to prevent killing the yeast)

2 eggs, lightly beaten

½ cup oil

½ cup milk

¼ cup sugar

1 teaspoon salt

5–6 cups flour, plus more as needed (I use organic unbleached flour to slow the process of starch turning to sugar in the digestion process)

2 tablespoons real butter, to brush over bread or rolls before baking

Instructions

1. Mix active dry yeast with 1 cup warm water and set aside to dissolve.

2. In a stand mixer with the dough hook attached or by hand with a wooden spoon, blend eggs, oil, and milk.

3. Add yeast and water mixture, and continue mixing as you add the sugar and salt.

4. Begin adding flour to the mixture with the dough hook in motion (or by hand), 1 cup at a time. Mixture will thicken as you add more. Once 4 cups are added, continue blending slowly until dough begins to form a ball, adding flour as needed. The dough should slightly clean the flour from sides of the bowl as you mix. The dough will be a bit sticky to the touch as you remove it from the bowl and/or dough hook.

5. Place the dough on a flat surface dusted with flour. Knead the dough by pressing it out into a circle, then lifting the sides and folding them back into the middle of the dough.

6. Form the dough into a large rectangular shape and place it into a large, greased glass bowl. Cover with a towel and set in a draft-free area.

7. After 45 minutes to 1 hour, the dough should have risen to double its original size. Punch the center of the dough and remove it from the bowl, back to the flour-dusted surface.

8. You may let it rest a few minutes, but I tend to be in a hurry most of my life, so I dig right in. Knead it again with more flour as needed.

9. Pull the dough apart into two pieces. Form each piece into a loaf and place in a greased loaf pan. Place the loaves in a draft-free area and let them rise until they are at least doubled in size.

10. When loaves have doubled in size, brush with melted butter and place in a preheated oven at 375°F.

11. Bake until loaves are nicely browned and sound hollow when tapped, about 40 minutes. You may wish to test this with a toothpick inserted inside of a loaf. If it comes out clean, it is ready.

12. Let set for a few minutes, then serve warm with fresh butter.

© Susie Winters

© Brenna Davis-Long, B. Davis Photography

Mom's No-Bake Cherry Cheesecake

My husband and I live on a farm in Central Oklahoma with our two dogs, Dally and Dot, two longhorns, and more cattle than I probably know of! We share our farm life as @frillyfarmcattleco on Instagram and invite you join us. This No-Bake Cherry Cheesecake has been a holiday staple on my mom's side of the family since I can remember. My mom taught me how to make it when I was very young, and I have been making it ever since. This is a super versatile recipe. Swap out the cherry pie filling for your favorite fruit filling to change the flavor.

Serves: 12 | Prep time: 25 minutes | Refrigerate: 2 hours

Ingredients

20 graham crackers, crushed

1¼ cups butter, melted

½ cup sugar, divided

2 (8-ounce) packages cream cheese, softened

1 teaspoon vanilla

Splash milk

2 (8-ounce) cans Cool Whip™, room temperature

2 (21-ounce) cans cherry pie filling

Instructions

1. Place graham crackers in large plastic bag and crush with a rolling pin.

2. Mix melted butter with the crushed graham crackers and ¼ cup sugar. Press to form a crust in a 9" × 13" pan.

3. In a large mixing bowl, combine the softened cream cheese, remaining sugar, vanilla, and milk and mix until combined. (Make sure that your cream cheese is softened before starting this step. If your cream cheese is too hard it can result in lumps in your cheesecake.)

4. Slowly add Cool Whip™ until well combined.

5. Spread an even layer of cream cheese mixture over the graham cracker crust.

6. Spoon cherry pie filling over the cream cheese mixture. Gently spread out the cherries to cover the entire pan.

7. Chill for at least 4 hours. Slice and enjoy!

© Heather Carter

Blackberry Pomegranate Jam

We have been cultivating Nature Hills Farm in the high desert of Cedar City, Utah, for over twelve years. We grow hundreds of varieties of fruits, herbs, and vegetables. We milk cows, raise chickens for eggs and meat, make cheese, breads, jams, and more. I grew up eating pomegranates and each year look forward to using the juice for some of our favorite jams. This recipe is one of Nature Hills Farm's signature jams as well as a crowd favorite.

Serves: 12 half pints | Prep time: 15 minutes | Cook time: 25–30 minutes | Processing time: 15 minutes

Ingredients

4 cups fresh or frozen blackberries, smashed

4 cups pomegranate juice

1 box powdered pectin

7 cups cane sugar

Instructions

1. Heat jars in simmering water until ready for use. Do not boil. Wash lids in warm soapy water and set bands aside.

2. Combine berries with pomegranate juice and pectin in a 6- or 8-quart saucepan.

3. Heat mixture until near boiling, then add sugar. Bring mixture to a full rolling boil that cannot be stirred down, over high heat, stirring frequently. Continue the hard boil for 1 minute, stirring constantly.

4. Remove from heat. Skim foam if necessary.

5. Ladle hot jam into hot jars, leaving ¼ inch headspace. Remove air bubbles and wipe jar rims. Center lids on jars and apply band. Place jar in boiling water canner. Repeat until all jars are filled.

6. Process jars in a in a pot of boiling water or a water-bath canner for 10 minutes. Turn off heat; remove lid and let stand for 5 minutes.

7. Remove jars and cool. Check lids for seal after 24 hours. Lid should not flex when the center is pressed.

Grandma's Breakfast Egg Dish

I am the CA Dairy Wife (http://cadairywife.com/) and a rich dairy-farming history runs in our family. My husband and I are both fourth-generation dairy farmers currently raising the fifth generation. We farm close to seven hundred acres and milk 2,100 cows in the Central Valley of California. I have chosen this delicious recipe to share with you all because it was and still is a staple dish for my husband and his family. I hope this dish will bless your family with as many memories as it has ours.

Serves: 8–10 | Prep time: 25 minutes | Cook time: 60–70 minutes

Ingredients

2 tablespoons chopped scallions

1 tablespoon butter, plus more for greasing the pan

6 eggs

3 cups whole milk

1½ cups cooked sausage

2 cups cheddar cheese

3 tablespoons flour

1 tablespoon dry mustard

3 cups French bread, no crust, cut into 1-inch squares

Instructions

1. Preheat oven to 350°F.

2. In a small frying pan, cook scallions in butter until slightly browned. Set aside.

3. In a large mixing bowl, beat eggs, then mix in milk, followed by cooked sausage, cheese, flour, dry mustard, cooked scallions, and French bread. Mix well.

4. Pour into a butter-coated 9" × 13" baking dish. Bake for 60 to 70 minutes.

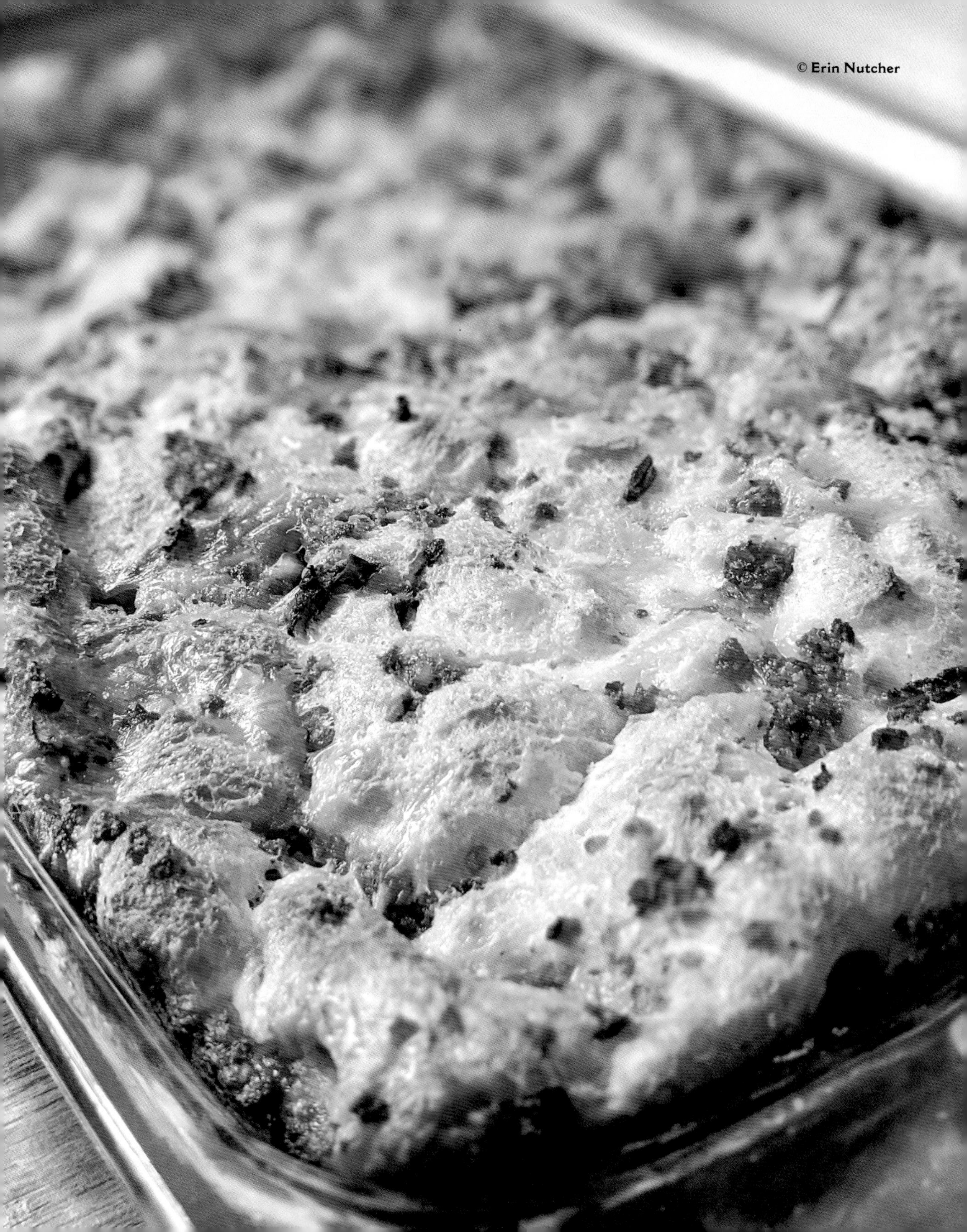

© Hannah Sons

Runamucka Ranch's "Better Than Anything" Brownies

We are the Wyld Sons Homestead residing in Northern Utah. We try to live life off the land, raising animals and growing our own food as much as possible, but sometimes you have to splurge and just eat the brownies! Many years ago, at Runamuka Ranch in the Bitterroot Valley of Montana, my mom these brownies to impress my dad. He was impressed, and so were others, leaving the rest to history! These brownies been made time and time again, serving many families and ranchers after a hard day's work.

Serves: 10   Prep time: 15 minutes | Cook time: 28 minutes

Ingredients

1 box German chocolate cake mix (or yellow cake mix)

¾ cup butter, melted

1 small can evaporated milk, divided

1 cup chopped walnuts or pecans

2 packages caramels (approximately 2 cups)

2 cups chocolate chips (or white chocolate if using yellow cake)

Instructions

1. Preheat your oven to 350°F. Grease a 9" × 11" glass pan or cast-iron skillet. Set aside.

2. In a bowl combine cake mix with melted butter, ½ can evaporated milk, and nuts. Pour half of this mixture into your glass pan or skillet and bake for 10 minutes.

3. While the first mixture is baking, melt the caramels and remaining evaporated milk together.

4. Pull first mixture out of the oven and sprinkle chocolate chips on top. Pour melted caramel on top of that, spreading evenly.

5. Scoop the remaining cake mixture evenly over melted caramel, covering the top. Put back in the oven and bake for 18 minutes.

6. Pull out of the oven and let cool. These brownies are good warm, but just as good cold.

© Hannah Sons

© Hannah Sons

Midwest Region

D & D Prime Rib

D&D Beef is a family-owned ranch located in Eastern Nebraska. We have been selling our ranch-raised beef to friends and family for over fifty years. We take great pride in our cattle and providing customers with beef from our ranch to their plate. This recipe is a family favorite around the holidays and special occasions and one that highlights the great natural flavor of beef.

Serves: 6 | Prep time: 24 hours | Cook time: 2½ hours

Ingredients

½ cup coarsely ground
   black pepper
½ teaspoon cardamom
1 tablespoon tomato paste
1 teaspoon paprika
½ teaspoon garlic powder
1 cup soy sauce
¾ cup vinegar
1 (6-pound) prime rib roast
   (bone-in can be used)

Instructions

1. Combine pepper and cardamom in mixing bowl. Use hands to rub mixture over all sides of beef.

2. In a separate bowl combine tomato paste, paprika, and garlic powder. Gradually add in soy sauce and vinegar.

3. Place prime rib in a large resealable bag or container. Then, add marinade to the same bag or container, being careful not to wash the rub off the meat. If placing in a bag, remove as much air as possible. Place beef in refrigerator to marinate overnight or up to 24 hours.

4. Baste the prime rib the next morning several times. If prime rib was placed in a bag overnight, carefully flip the prime rib over to marinate the other side.

5. Remove prime rib from the marinade approximately 1 hour prior to cooking and let sit at room temperature. Preheat oven to 450°F.

6. Sear meat for 15 minutes, then lower oven temperature to 275°F to 300°F. Cook for approximately 2 hours to desired wellness. Prime rib will take 13 to 15 minutes per pound. (Rule of thumb: Remove from oven 5°F to 10°F before desired doneness.)

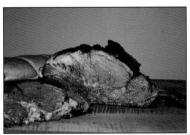

© Michaela Mann

7. When desired doneness is reached, remove from oven and loosely tent with foil. Allow prime rib to rest approximately 20 minutes prior to carving.

Summer Vegetable Quiche

A warm welcome from the Wilsons at the Little Pallet Farmhouse! Our family of five sold it all and moved to rural Missouri where we now live the beautifully exhausting, challenging, and rewarding farm life. Follow us on YouTube (www.youtube.com/thelittlepalletfarmhouse) as we learn old-fashioned traditions and work together as a family to pursue our homestead dreams. I also host the Homestead Documentary series which features the lives of other homesteaders all over the USA who share their stories of how they produce, provide, and profit from the land that they live on. This summer vegetable quiche is one of the ways we enjoy the bounty from our summer garden and home-farmed eggs as a simple, satisfying, and versatile meal.

Serves: 8 | Prep time: 30 minutes | Cook time: 45–55 minutes

Ingredients

Pie Crust (9-inch)

2½ cups flour

½ teaspoon salt

1 stick (8 tablespoons) butter, plus extra for greasing the dish

½ cup sour cream

Filling*

1 tablespoon extra-virgin olive oil

4 small red bell peppers, deseeded and sliced

3 banana shallots, finely chopped

4 tablespoons grape jelly

2 tablespoons balsamic vinegar

Quiche

4 large organic eggs

½ cup whole milk

½ cup heavy cream

¼ teaspoon salt

¼ teaspoon pepper

½ cup shredded cheese

2 cups filling

1 beefsteak tomato, for topping)

2 tablespoons basil pesto, for topping

* Filling alternatives include spinach, mushrooms, broccoli, asparagus, sweet potato, or any other cooked, roasted, or sautéed vegetables of your choice.

(continued on page 69)

Instructions

Pie Crust

1. Preheat oven to 375°F. Grease a 9" × 9" quiche dish with butter.

2. In a large mixing bowl combine flour, salt, and remaining butter, rubbing with fingertips until resembling texture of fine bread crumbs. Add in sour cream and mix to form a ball of pastry dough. If you are making your pastry dough in advance, after this step you can store in fridge or freezer in plastic wrap.

3. On a floured surface, roll out your pastry dough to fit a 9" × 9" quiche dish. Bake at 375°F for 10 to 15 minutes.

4. Remove from oven, pat down any air bubbles using the back of a wooden spoon, and set aside to cool.

Filling

1. Heat the olive oil in a skillet on medium-high heat. Add peppers and shallots and cook until soft. Continue cooking until any liquid from the vegetables has evaporated.

2. Add grape jelly and balsamic vinegar. Keep stirring over medium heat until vegetables are glazed in sauce.

3. Set aside in a dish to cool. (You can freeze surplus filling or use it next day on homemade pizza—yum!)

Quiche

1. In a mixing bowl add all quiche ingredients and stir together to combine.

2. Add two cups filling to cover the pastry base of quiche.

3. Pour in quiche mixture to cover filling. This should fill remaining space in quiche tin.

4. Top with slices of tomato and dots of pesto.

5. Bake at 350°F for 45 to 55 minutes.

Farmhouse Cheeseburger Soup

I live on seven acres in Missouri, in an 1860s farmhouse, with my husband and six kids. We spend our days homeschooling, cooking, homesteading, and making content for our blog, Farmhouse on Boone, YouTube *channel, and podcast. Cheeseburger Soup is a healthy, protein-packed dish, perfect for an easy weeknight meal. It is a favorite in our family, and the perfect cozy way to sneak bone broth and vegetables into our winter diet.*

Serves: 6 | Prep time: 10 minutes | Cook time: 20 minutes

Ingredients

5 large potatoes, chopped
5 carrots, diced
2 onions, diced
5 stalks celery, diced
5 cloves garlic, minced
6 cups chicken broth
   (homemade is preferable)
2 pounds ground beef,
   browned
2 teaspoons dried parsley
3 teaspoons salt
Several grindings fresh
   black pepper
10 ounces cheddar cheese,
   shredded
Avocado, sour cream,
   fresh herbs, croutons, or
   fermented pickles, for
   topping

Instructions

1. Add all the veggies and broth to a 5-quart cast-iron Dutch oven and bring to a boil. Reduce the heat to low and allow it to simmer for about 20 minutes.

2. In a skillet, brown the ground beef. Then, add it to the Dutch oven. Add parsley, salt, and pepper.

3. Add the shredded cheddar.

4. Add toppings. Our favorites include: avocado, sour cream, fresh herbs, croutons, or even some fermented pickles. (What is a cheeseburger without pickles?)

© Lisa Bass

© Erin Blegen

Wild Blueberry Scones

At Yellow Birch Hobby Farm here in Northeast Minnesota, my husband Josh and I, along with our three kids, have carved out a from-scratch lifestyle that focuses on raising, growing, hunting, and gathering as much of our own food as possible. That includes foraging for wild blueberries every summer when the land gives up its bounty. This Wild Blueberry Scones recipe is a favorite that we have enjoyed hundreds of times.

Serves: 8 | Prep time: 20 minutes | Cook time: 18 minutes

Ingredients

Scones
½ heaping cup full fat sour cream
1 large egg
1 teaspoon vanilla extract
2 cups all-purpose flour
1 tablespoon baking powder
½ cup sugar
¼ teaspoon salt
½ cup (1 stick) cold butter, cut into 8 pieces
Zest of 1 lemon
1 cup fresh or frozen wild blueberries (if using frozen, do not thaw)
Coarse cane sugar for sprinkling on top

Glaze
1 tablespoon butter, melted
1–2 tablespoons milk
1 teaspoon vanilla extract
¼–½ cup powdered sugar

Instructions
1. Preheat oven to 400°F.
2. In a small bowl whisk together the sour cream, egg, and vanilla until smooth. Set aside.
3. In a large bowl or food processor combine the flour, baking powder, sugar, and salt. Add in the cold butter and pulse in a food processor or by hand with a pastry blender or fork until the mixture is sandy and only pea-sized pieces remain. If using a food processor, transfer to a large bowl.
4. Make a well in the middle of the dough mixture and pour in the wet ingredients. Working gently with a silicone spatula, fold the ingredients together, being careful not to overwork the dough. Stop mixing just as soon as the mixture is combined (it should appear shaggy).
5. Add the lemon zest and blueberries; gently fold together just until combined.
6. Pour the contents out onto a lightly floured table or pastry mat and bring it together into an 8-inch round. Use a sharp knife or bench scraper to divide the round into 8 triangles.
7. Transfer the scones to a parchment-lined half cookie sheet, spacing them at least 2 inches apart. Sprinkle coarse cane sugar over the top of each scone. Bake for 18 minutes; remove from the oven to cool in the pan for 10 to 15 minutes.
8. Meanwhile, prepare the glaze by whisking together the melted butter, milk, and vanilla. Gradually add in the powdered sugar, ¼ cup at a time, until you have reached the desired consistency. Drizzle over the scones and serve.

Baker Creek Nasturtium Pesto

I founded Baker Creek Heirloom Seed Co. in 1998 with the simple desire to save and share open-pollinated, heirloom varieties that have been passed down from generation to generation in families and communities. Part of Baker Creek's mission is to protect seed diversity and security in an age of corporate agriculture and patented, hybridized, or genetically modified seeds. We also love exploring the flavors and uses of these beautiful plants, including nasturtiums. They are known for their bright colors that can light up any garden, but these hardy annuals are also deliciously versatile and packed with nutrition. The mildly peppery flavor of nasturtium leaves offers a tasty twist on traditional basil pesto, and the pesto's creamy texture is reminiscent of guacamole! We use the leaves of Cherry Rose Jewel nasturtiums, but any variety will work well.

Serves: 8–12 | Prep time: 10 minutes

Ingredients

5 cups clean nasturtium
   leaves, loosely packed
⅓ cup walnuts
5 cloves garlic
½ cup olive oil
½ cup vegan Parmesan
½ teaspoon salt
¼ teaspoon pepper
1 tablespoon lemon juice

Instructions

1. Fill your blender or food processor to about ¾ full with nasturtium leaves. Blend leaves until they are roughly chopped. Add more leaves, blend.

2. Add in the walnuts and blend.

3. Add in the remaining ingredients and blend.

4. Adjust seasonings to taste.

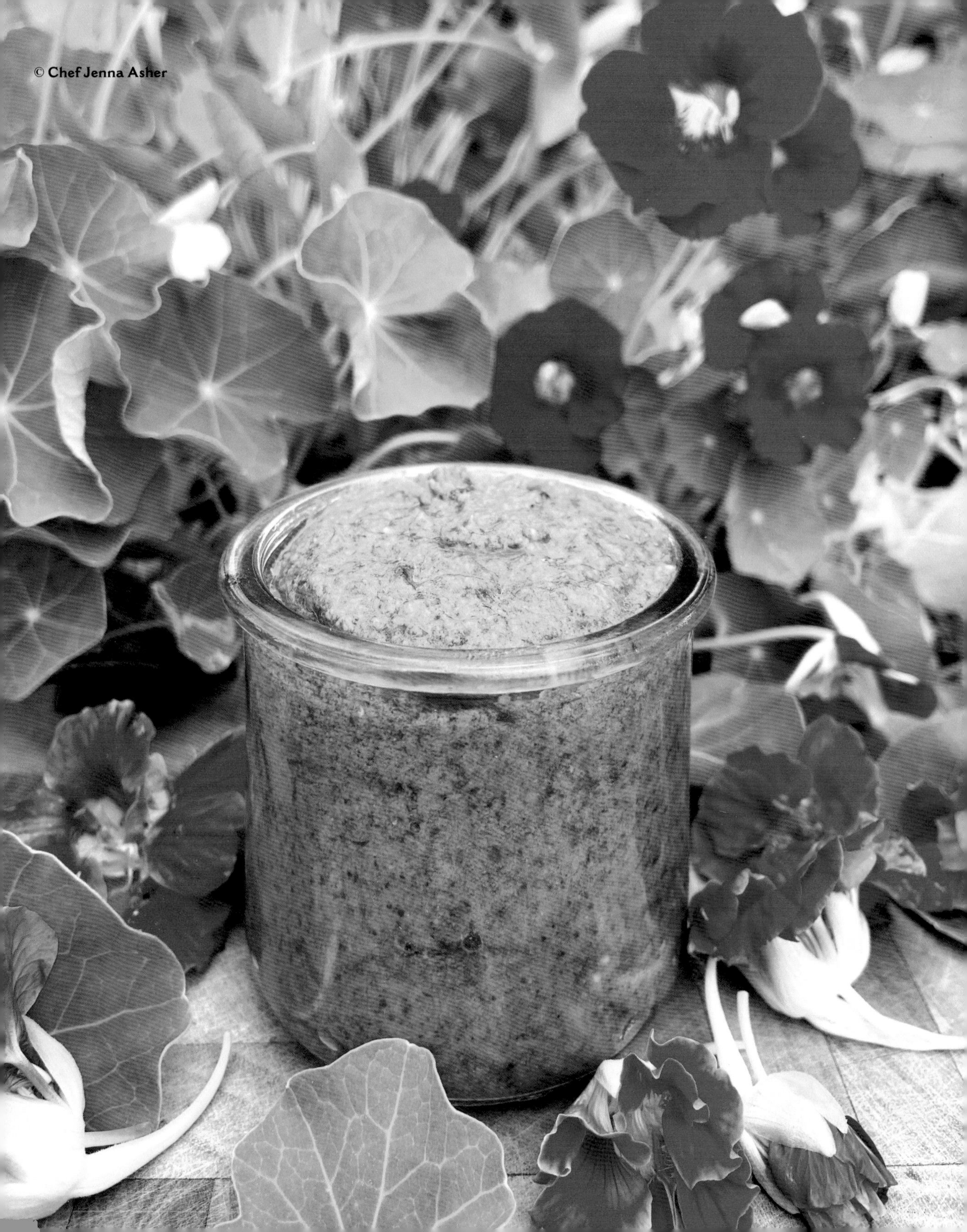

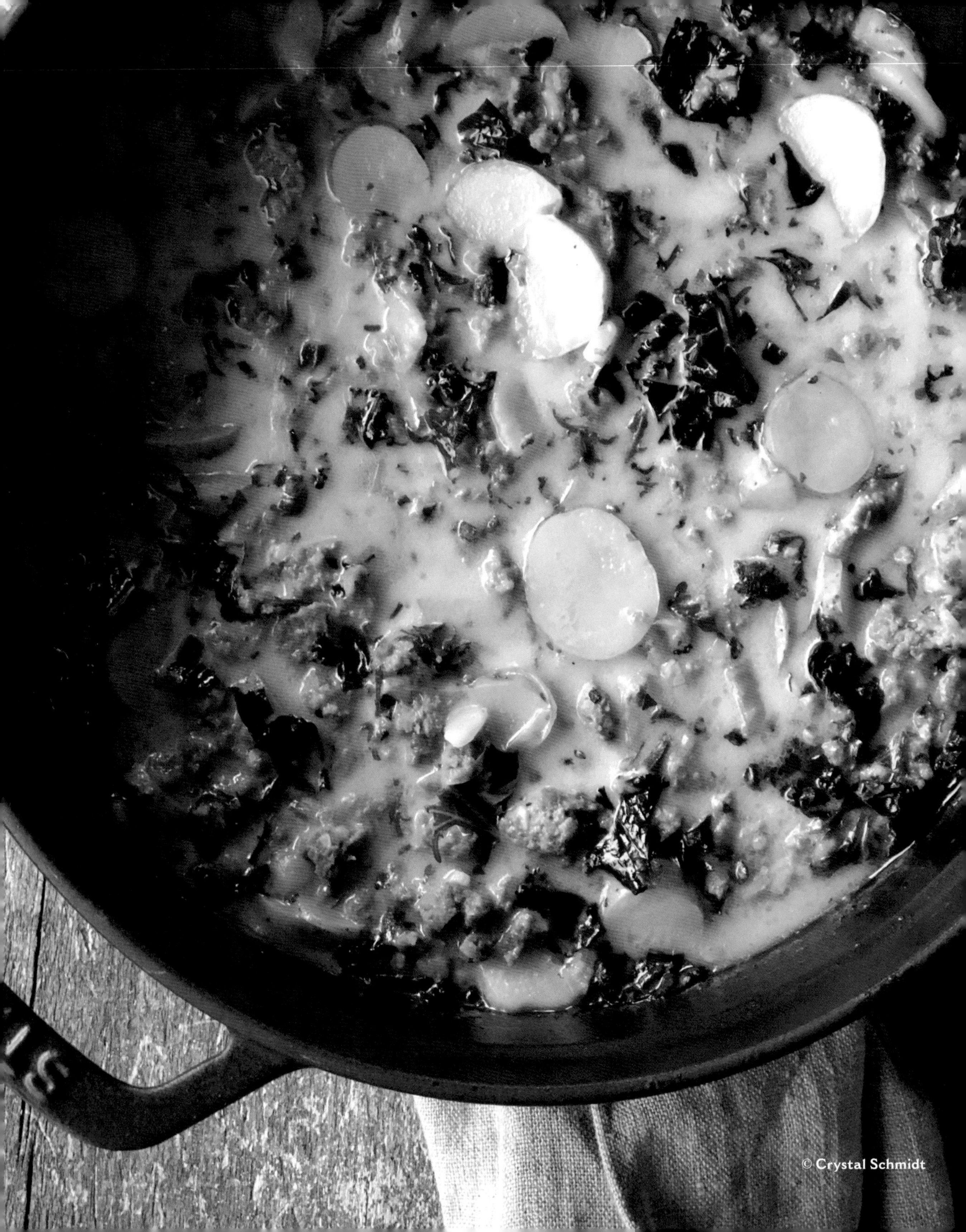

Creamy Sausage, Potato, and Kale Soup

One of my earliest memories is from when I was just a little girl, sitting in the dirt in my grandma's garden while she weeded. She had a huge garden full of beautiful produce, and she had a special love of growing kale. Of course, she taught my dad to garden, and he taught me. Wanting to grow food has always come from a deep place, and once you've tasted something you've raised yourself with a whole lotta heart and soul . . . well, nothing else even comes close! I chronicle my home-cooked, handmade, and homegrown lifestyle as @wholefedhomestead on Instagram. My soup recipe is a family favorite that pays homage to my upbringing with a hearty helping of kale, which is now one of my favorite veggies to grow too!

Serves: 4–6 | Prep time: 10 minutes | Cook time: 40 minutes

Ingredients

2 pounds pork sausage
1 tablespoon olive oil
1 medium onion, diced
3 ribs celery, diced
4 cups chicken broth
Salt and pepper, to taste
2 cups fingerling potatoes,
   thinly sliced
2 cloves garlic, minced
2 teaspoons dried parsley
1 teaspoon dried sage
½ teaspoon dried thyme
½ teaspoon dried rosemary
4 cups chopped kale,
   center ribs removed
½ cup heavy cream
Finely grated Parmesan
   cheese, for serving

Instructions

1. Brown the pork sausage and drain the excess fat; set the sausage aside.

2. In a medium-sized pot, heat olive oil and sauté the onion and celery until softened, about 5 to 8 minutes. Add in the chicken broth and cooked sausage, then bring to a simmer. Since everyone's broth and sausage may be different, taste to see if it needs salt and pepper, and season to taste before proceeding to the next step.

3. Add in the fingerling potatoes, garlic, and all the dried herbs. Simmer over medium heat, stirring occasionally, for 15 minutes or until the potatoes are tender.

4. Add in the kale and simmer for 3 minutes more. Turn off the heat and stir in the heavy cream.

5. Ladle into bowls and top each bowl with a sprinkle of Parmesan cheese.

Farmhouse Sourdough Bread

Ashley Marie Farm and Bakery is a small homestead in Midwest Michigan where we hope to pass down a love of crafting good food and good land with our own hands. This is the loaf we bake weekly for our children to enjoy. It is perfect for toast, sandwiches, or just slathered with butter fresh from the oven!

Serves: 2 loaves | Prep time: 1 hour active, up to 20 hours inactive | Cook time: 20–30 minutes

Ingredients
1¾ cups milk
4 tablespoons sugar
4 tablespoons butter, melted
1 teaspoon salt
3½ cups bread or all-purpose flour
¾ cup Simple Sourdough Starter (recipe on page 80)

Instructions
1. Place all ingredients into a large bowl. Mix thoroughly until all ingredients are incorporated and you have a shaggy dough.

2. Cover and let rest for 20 to 30 minutes.

3. After the rest period, knead the dough in the bowl by folding the dough in half over onto itself for about 5 to 10 minutes. It will be a bit sticky but do not add more flour.

4. Cover and let rest again for 20 to 30 minutes.

5. Next, dump the dough onto an un-floured surface and knead again for 5 to 10 minutes. It should be less sticky now and leave a mostly clean counter. It should ever so slightly stick to your fingers. If it is still very sticky, let it rest and knead again.

6. Place the dough back into the bowl, cover, and let rise until the dough doubles size, about 8 to 10 hours.

7. Once the dough is doubled in size, dump dough out onto a floured surface and divide in half.

8. Shape the two halves of dough into logs, then place into two lightly greased 5" × 8" bread pans. Cover with plastic or place in a plastic bag and let rise again until the dough doubles in size, about 8 to 10 hours.

9. When the loaves have risen to about ½-inch over the top of the bread pan, preheat the oven to 375°F. Once oven is preheated, bake loaves for 20 to 30 minutes or until golden brown on top.

10. Remove from oven and let cool for 5 minutes, then remove from bread pans to finish cooling. Enjoy!

Simple Sourdough Starter

Ashley Marie Farm and Bakery is a small homestead in Midwest Michigan where we hope to pass down a love of crafting good food and good land with our own hands. We chose to share this recipe with you because historically when packaged yeast was not available our ancestors would turn to their sourdough starters to bring fresh, tasty bread to the table.

Serves: 1 cup | Prep time: 3–5 days

Ingredients

½ cup flour, plus more as needed

½ cup water, plus more as needed

Instructions

1. Place the flour and water in a quart-sized mason jar or equivalent and stir until well mixed. Cover with a loose lid and leave at room temperature for 8 hours.

2. After 8 hours, scoop out approximately ½ of the flour/water mixture and compost or throw it in the garbage (or use the discard for another recipe like Sourdough Noodles on page 106). Then, again add ½ cup flour and ½ cup water to the remaining mixture in the jar and stir until well mixed. Cover and leave for another 8 hours.

3. Repeat discarding ½ of the mixture and feeding it more flour and water every 8 hours for approximately 3 to 5 days.

4. After 3 to 5 days, your starter should be rising to double its size, showing bubbles, and smelling slightly sour or yeasty. This is when you know it is ready to be used. If it isn't there yet, continue feeding it (be sure to discard half before feeding!) until it is doubling and bubbly.

5. Once your starter is doubling and bubbling consistently, place it in the fridge until you are ready to bake with it, taking it out 8 hours beforehand and feeding it.

Lamb Shepherd's Pie

Our family resides in Northwest Indiana on Stoner Family Farms. I created this recipe years ago when we started raising lambs. My family loves this comfort meal on a cold fall or wintry day. I also make it every St. Patrick's Day, topped with colcannon* (cooked cabbage mixed in with mashed potatoes). We pride ourselves in using resources from our farm and this dish represents who we are and what we do!

Serves: 6–8 | Prep time: 30 minutes | Cook time: 20 minutes

Ingredients

Filling

2 pounds ground lamb or ground beef
2 cups carrots, peeled and diced
1½ cups frozen sweet corn
1 cup frozen green peas
2 cloves garlic, smashed
1 teaspoon dried parsley
½ teaspoon dried rosemary
½ teaspoon thyme
½ teaspoon marjoram
½ teaspoon oregano
Salt and pepper, to taste

Sauce

1½ cups beef broth
2 tablespoons flour
2 tablespoons tomato paste
Worcestershire sauce, to taste
Salt and pepper, to taste

Toppings

4 cups cooked mashed potatoes
½ cup cheddar cheese
Fresh parsley, chopped (optional)

Instructions

1. Preheat oven to 350°F.

2. For the filling, in a large cast iron skillet, add ground lamb and cook on high until browned.

3. Meanwhile, place the carrots in a microwave-safe bowl. Microwave on high to soften, or partially cook, for approximately 3 minutes. (To cut down on the prep time of this recipe swap the fresh carrots, frozen sweet corn, and frozen peas for a bag of mixed frozen vegetables from your local grocery store.)

* To make colcannon, simply add 2 cups cooked cabbage to the cooked potatoes you will be mashing.

(continued on page 83)

4. Once the lamb is fully browned, add the carrots, corn, peas, and garlic to the skillet. Cook on medium heat for approximately 5 minutes or until all the vegetables are fully cooked. Then, add the spices.

5. For the sauce, place the beef broth, flour, tomato paste, and Worcestershire sauce in a small bowl. Add salt and pepper to taste and whisk well.

6. Add the sauce mixture to the filling mixture. Cook on medium to low heat for approximately 5 minutes until the mixture thickens and begins to bubble.

7. Top the lamb mixture with cooked mashed potatoes, cheese, and parsley.

8. Bake for approximately 20 minutes or until the top gets brown and cheese the is melted.

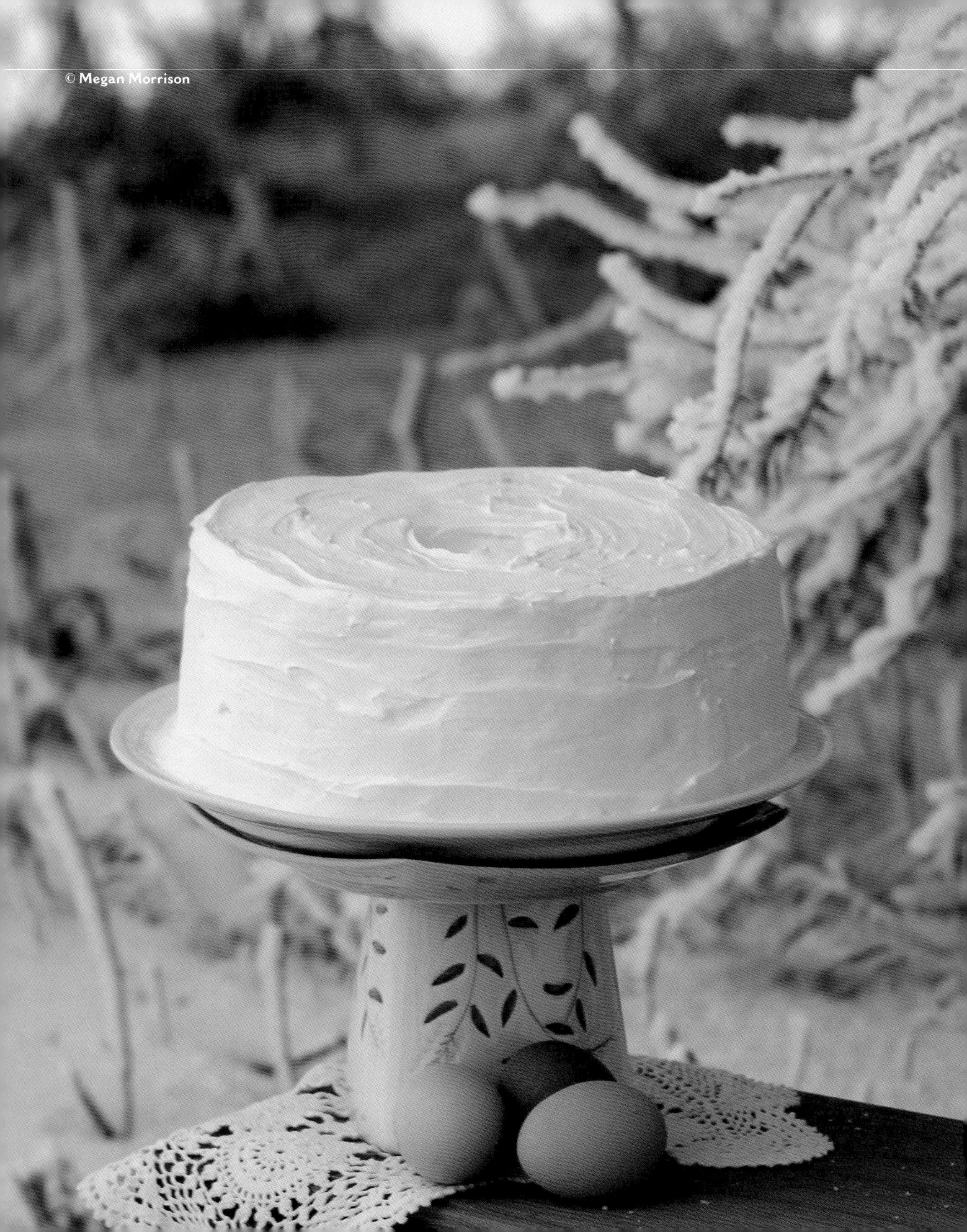

Grandma's Angel Food Cake

This Angel Food Cake recipe has been passed down from my grandmother (Clara Wolff) and was a staple for every birthday she celebrated. Birthdays with Grandma hold a special place in my heart, as I was her "seventieth birthday present," born just two days before. Famous for its thirteen egg whites, this cake will always fluff best with farm-fresh eggs. Here at Homestead on the Hill, we now have chickens to make the fluffiest Angel Food Cake! Serve with your favorite topping or enjoy it plain . . . smiles are always included!

Serves: 16 | Prep time: 12 minutes | Cook time: 55 minutes

Ingredients

Angel Food Cake
1 cup sifted cake flour
1½ cups sugar, divided
13 (about 1¼ cups)
  egg whites at room
  temperature*
¼ teaspoon salt
1½ teaspoons cream of
  tartar
1 teaspoon vanilla extract
1 teaspoon almond extract

Seven-Minute Frosting
2 egg whites
1½ cups sugar
¼ teaspoon cream of tartar
⅓ cup water
1 teaspoon vanilla extract

Instructions

1. Preheat the oven to 325°F.

2. For the cake, sift together three times: cake flour and ½ cup sugar.

3. In a separate bowl, beat egg whites and salt at medium speed until frothy.

4. Add the cream of tartar to the egg whites and beat at high speed until stiff, but not dry.

5. Gradually add 1 cup sugar to egg whites while mixing at a low speed. Beat only until sugar is blended, scraping the sides of the bowl frequently with a rubber spatula.

6. Add the vanilla extract, almond extract, and flour/sugar mixture to the egg whites, mixing at a low speed.

7. Turn the mix into an ungreased 10" × 10" tube pan. Bake for 30 to 45 minutes, or until the top is golden brown.

8. Turn cake upside down to cool. Do not remove from the pan until cool.

9. For the frosting, preheat a double boiler by adding water and bringing to a slow rolling boil.

* Remove eggs from refrigerator several hours before using or use fresh eggs that have not been chilled.

(continued on next page)

10. Combine the egg whites, sugar, cream of tartar, and water in the top pan of a double boiler. Beat mixture on high speed for 1 minute.

11. Place the top pot with the mixture over the boiling water (water should not touch the top pan) and beat on high speed for 7 minutes.

12. Remove top pan from heat.

13. Add vanilla and beat for 2 minutes on high speed.

14. Frost your cake once it has cooled.

Apple Pie Popovers

Everbrooke Farms is a small family farm established in 1900. It's nestled down a long dirt road in a quaint Michigan town of only three hundred people. With a cozy white farmhouse, large wraparound porch, and historic red barns, it is the perfect place for our family to raise mini pigs, mini bunnies, horses, fluffy chickens, and turkeys. Whether for early morning breakfast or late-night desserts, these easy Apple Pie Popovers are a treat for all. We hope that you enjoy this farm-to-table dish as much as we do.

Serves: 6 | Prep time: 10 minutes | Cook time: 40 minutes

Ingredients

4 large eggs
1 cup milk
¼ teaspoon salt
1 cup bread flour
2 tablespoons softened butter
20 ounces apple pie filling
Whipped cream, for topping
    (optional)

© Erin Williamson

Instructions

1. Preheat oven to 425°F.

2. In a medium bowl with a whisk or whisk attachment, beat the eggs, milk, and salt together. Beat in the bread flour, a little at a time, until it is completely smooth.

3. Grease the insides of popover cups or a muffin tin with butter. If you are using an extra-large muffin pan, grease every other cup.

4. Divide the apple pie filling, putting an equal amount in the bottom of each cup.

5. Pour the batter over the filling, filling the cups half full.

6. Bake at 425°F for 20 minutes. Then, reduce the heat to 350°F and continue baking for 15 minutes, until popovers are slightly golden on top.

© Erin Williamson

© Erin Williamson

(continued on next page)

© Erin Williamson

7. Turn the oven off and let the popovers stand in the oven for 10 to 12 minutes or until they are firm enough to avoid collapsing.

8. Remove the popovers from the oven. Lift the popovers from the pan immediately and place them on a serving dish.

9. After cooling slightly, add a dollop of whipped cream, if desired, before serving.

Bison Pot Roast

Nestled along the Missouri River is our Buffalo Coulee Ranch. This ranch, homesteaded over one hundred years ago, has been a traditional family farm raising cattle and chickens, milking cows, and farming the land. Bison Pot Roast has become a staple on our family table. With busy schedules, it is easy to prepare and at the end of a long workday the smell in the kitchen is mouthwatering. Enjoy!

Serves: 6 | Prep time: 20 minutes | Cook time: 8 hours

Ingredients

4–5 pounds bison chuck roast

2 teaspoons kosher salt

1 teaspoon coarse ground black pepper

1 pound (5 medium) carrots, peeled and cut into 2-inch chunks

1 pound (4–5 medium) red potatoes, cut into large chunks

2 cloves garlic, finely grated

2 cups low-sodium beef broth (1 can beer may be substituted)

Instructions

1. Season the chuck roast with kosher salt and pepper.

2. In your slow cooker, add the carrots, potatoes, and garlic.

3. Lay the bison on top, then add the beef broth or can of beer and cover, cooking on low for 8 to 10 hours or on high for 5 to 6 hours. Note: cooking times may vary, so adjust your slow cooker accordingly.

© Ruth Mclachlan

Farmhouse Granola

We came to Belvedere Farms in search of good, wholesome, nutrient-dense food. We work hard, eat well, spend long days outside, and wouldn't have it any other way. Our milk cow Sandy gives a lot of milk (three to five gallons a day!). Coupled with this farmhouse granola, it's a quick and hearty breakfast full of all the good things that will keep your energy high so you can make progress on that mile-long list of farm projects. The beauty of this recipe is that the flavors can be adapted to anything you have on hand. These are some of our favorites: almonds, cranberries, and dried apple chips; walnuts and dried cherries; almonds and dried blueberries; pecans and dried apricots; walnuts and dried banana chips.

Serves: 12 cups | Prep time: 10 minutes | Cook time: 20 minutes

Ingredients

4½ cups oatmeal

½ cup oatmeal flour*

1 teaspoon salt

½ cup milled flaxseed

1¼ cups nuts of your choice, chopped

2½ cups dried fruit of your choice

½ cup honey

½ cup coconut oil, melted

Instructions

1. Preheat oven to 350°F. Combine all ingredients in a large mixing bowl.

2. Spread in an even layer on a parchment-covered baking sheet.

3. Bake for 10 minutes. Stir. Bake 10 minutes more.

4. Remove from the oven. Let cool on the baking sheet. Store in an airtight container.

* Oatmeal flour improves the texture of this granola, but there's no need to purchase additional ingredients. Just pulse regular oatmeal in a food processor, blender, or spice grinder.

Fangboner Fried Shrimp
with Broccoli and Spiced Rice

Fangboner Farms is a family-owned Ohio farm established in 2012 and run by the Richardson family. We grow all our own herbs, then dry them to create our tantalizing signature blends. This recipe uses the herbs grown on our farm today and is a replica of the southern home cooking that Elizabeth, our CEO, was raised on.

Serves: 3 | Prep time: 10 minutes | Cook time: 15 minutes

Ingredients

Rice
1 cup long-grain rice
1½–2 cups water (enough to cover long-grain rice)
1–2 tablespoons extra-virgin olive oil
1 tablespoon Yum Spice (or substitute for Fabflava Rub)

Broccoli
1 tablespoon extra-virgin olive oil
4 cups fresh broccoli
1 cup sliced onion
Salt, to taste

Shrimp
½ cup coconut milk
Salt, to taste
1 tablespoon Yum Spice, plus more to taste
1 pound large peeled, deveined shrimp
½ cup plain protein powder (substitute with almond flour, coconut flour, or other flour of choice)
Oil, for frying

Instructions

1. For rice, add long-grain rice and water to a pot of boiling water or an Instant Pot. If using a pot, cook rice according to package instructions. If using an Instant Pot, cover and set to high pressure for 4 minutes.

2. If using a pot, turn off heat. If using an Instant Pot, release pressure. Add olive oil, Yum Spice (or substitute for Fabflava Rub), and mix until combined.

3. For broccoli, in a skillet add 1 tablespoon olive oil and turn heat to high. Add the broccoli and sauté for 4 to 6 minutes. Add the onion and sauté with broccoli until translucent. Add salt to taste.

4. For shrimp, add coconut milk, salt, Yum Spice, and shrimp to a large bowl and let it sit for 10 minutes.

5. Season the protein powder or flour with more Yum Spice to taste.

6. Remove the shrimp from milk mixture and coat well with the seasoned powder. Be sure to coat the shrimp really well with the seasoned powder. The shrimp shouldn't be seen once coated.

7. Fry the shrimp for 4 minutes or until crispy in oil. The oil should be around 375°F.

8. Remove the shrimp from the oil onto a paper towel-lined plate. Place shrimp on top of rice and broccoli. Serve immediately. Enjoy!

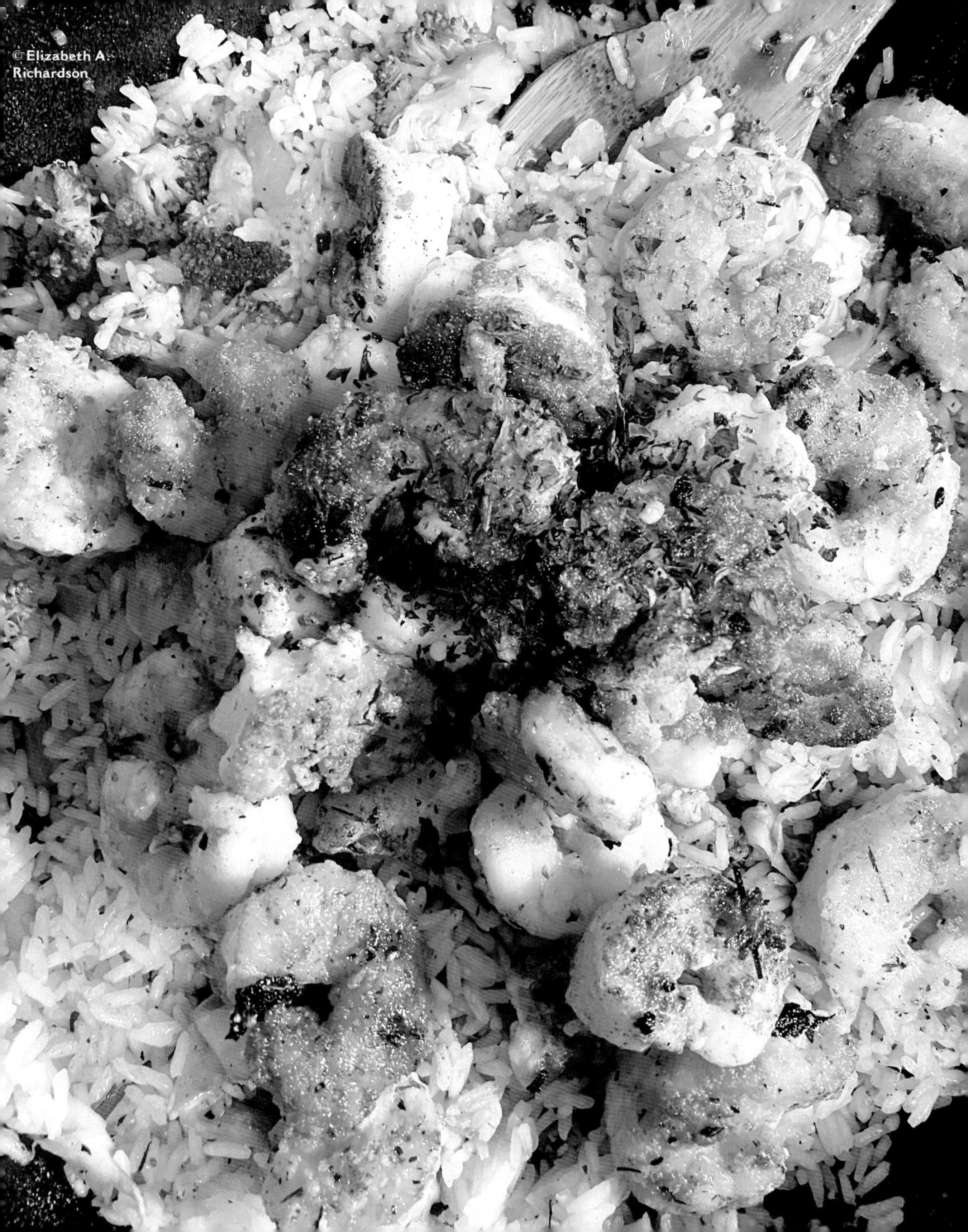

© Jennie Anderson, Bluestone Ranch

Garlic and Honey Meatballs

Bluestone Ranch is a small, diversified ranch with pigs, chickens, and about one hundred Scottish Highland cattle that graze in the rolling hills and prairie around our home in North Dakota. We are a busy family and enjoy preparing simple, nutritious meals. This is a recipe the entire family will love; our six ranch kids ask for this meal frequently! Serve these scrumptious meatballs on top of mashed potatoes. This pairs well with roasted carrots and a slice of homemade farm bread.

Serves: 6–8

Ingredients
2 pounds ground beef
1 cup quick rolled oats (can substitute equal amounts bread crumbs)
2 eggs
½ cup milk
1 teaspoon garlic powder
1 teaspoon garlic salt
4 cloves garlic, pressed
1 cup ketchup
⅔ cup honey
3 tablespoons soy sauce

Instructions
1. Preheat oven to 375°F.

2. Mix together ground beef, oats, eggs, milk, and garlic powder and salt.

3. Form meatballs and place on cooking sheet lined with parchment paper.

4. Cook for 30 to 35 minutes until meatballs are no longer pink in the middle.

5. While meatballs are cooking, prepare the sauce: place pressed garlic cloves, ketchup, honey, and soy sauce in a saucepan and heat through.

6. Add meatballs to sauce, toss, and serve!

© Jena Ochsner

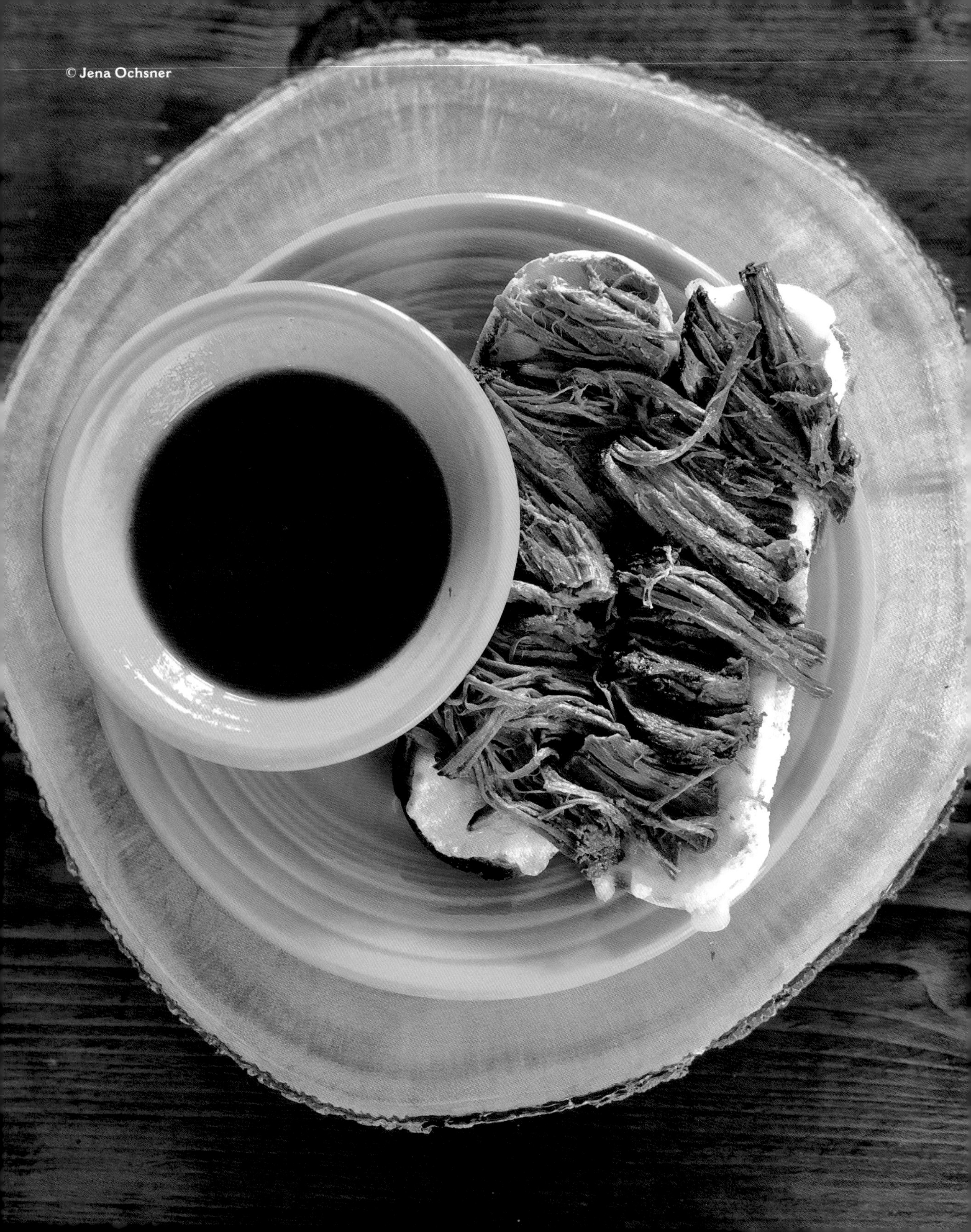

French Dip Sandwiches

Our family has been raising cows and crops in small-town Nebraska since 1885. We, along with our two boys, live on the original family homestead that is nestled just outside of Sutton, Nebraska, and is home base for all things Double O Farms. Our beef is homegrown right here on our farm and then dry aged for several weeks to produce the best beef you've ever tasted. We ship our beef nationwide and are proud to have a homegrown product on tables all across the country. These beef roast French Dip Sandwiches are a staple for our hardworking family!

Serves: 6–8 | Prep time: 10 minutes | Cook time: 10–12 hours

Ingredients

1 large beef roast

2 cups water

Seasoning of choice for the
   roast, plus more to taste
   (I like to use Nature's or
   Montreal Steak)

1 teaspoon garlic powder

Butter, for buns

Buns of choice (I like to use
   artisan sausage rolls)

Swiss cheese, for layering

Instructions

1. Place roast in crock pot with water. Season with seasoning of choice and garlic powder. Cook on low for 10 to 12 hours.

2. Butter buns and lightly season with more Nature's or garlic powder. Layer swiss cheese slices. Broil in oven until cheese is melted and buns are slightly crispy on the edges, about 3 minutes.

3. Add desired amount of beef roast on bun and dip in au jus if desired. Enjoy!

New England Region

© Suzanne Lee

Cape Cod Select's Cranberry Chutney

Cape Cod Select is a woman-owned premium cranberry and fruit company based in Carver, Massachusetts. We had always wondered why you couldn't find whole frozen cranberries year-round like you could mango, dragon fruit, and other out of season fruits. Knocking on grocery retailers' doors and sharing our passion for whole healthy cranberries to all who listened, we made it our mission to make this super fruit available to consumers year-round. Cape Cod Select is now the top selling retail brand in frozen cranberries. We chose to share this recipe because it is traditional to cranberries but also not your traditional cranberry sauce. Adding spices and apple make this a unique blend of warm flavors that pair perfectly with pork and poultry, mixed into yogurt, or served over warm brie and vanilla ice cream!

Serves: 8 | Prep time: 5 minutes | Cook time: 20 minutes

Ingredients

4 cups Cape Cod Select frozen cranberries
1 large tart apple, chopped in ½-inch cubes or smaller
½ cup sugar
½ cup honey
1 cup water
1 teaspoon cinnamon
1 teaspoon ground ginger
½ teaspoon ground cloves

Instructions

1. Combine all ingredients in a medium saucepan.

2. Bring to a boil, stirring frequently.

3. Reduce heat and simmer for 15 to 20 minutes until the apple is tender and the mixture thickens.

4. Transfer chutney into a resealable container and allow to cool before placing in the fridge. Chutney will keep for 2 weeks in fridge.

Baked Venison Meatballs

I grew up on Timber Creek Farm and learned to cook alongside my mom, farmer and writer Janet Garman. With a husband who enjoys hunting, and a growing family, I had plenty of opportunity to create new versions of standard recipes using game as the main ingredient. Meatballs are a versatile main dish or appetizer, equally enjoyed by kids and adults. Of course, you can use Baked Venison Meatballs in the traditional favorite method, served over spaghetti and marinara sauce. They are also delicious served with a sweet and sour sauce, a pizza sauce on crusty rolls for meatball sandwiches, and can even take the place of stew meat in savory stews and soups.

Serves: 20–25 meatballs | Prep tim: 15 minutes | Cook time: 30 minutes

Ingredients

1 pound ground venison or ground bison

2 eggs

1 cup Panko-style bread crumbs

1 teaspoon garlic powder or 1–2 cloves fresh garlic, minced

2 tablespoons Italian herb seasoning blend

½ cup Parmesan cheese (trust me, you will not regret adding this!)

Instructions

1. Preheat oven to 350°F.

2. Combine all ingredients in a large mixing bowl and mix well.

3. Roll mixture into 1-inch balls and place on a baking sheet.

4. Bake for 30 minutes. Roll meatballs over at 15 minutes if you prefer them evenly browned and not flat.

5. To freeze for later, arrange the meatballs on a wax paper–lined cookie sheet. Place in the freezer. Once the meatballs are frozen, transfer to a freezer container or freezer bag.

© Janet Garman

Sourdough Noodles

I own and operate Wild Way Farm & Apiary, a small farm focusing on biodynamic gardening, soil health, and self-reliant living in New Hampshire. Established in 2012, we grow heirloom vegetables, have many perennial pollinator gardens, and are developing a zone 5 fruit forest. This is our go-to pasta recipe for using up leftover sourdough discard that would otherwise be wasted.

Serves: 4 | Prep time: 30 minutes | Resting time: 8 hours | Cook time: 5 minutes

Ingredients

1 cup discard of Simple Sourdough Starter (recipe on page 80)
3 cups flour
6 egg yolks

Instructions

1. Pour sourdough starter into mixing bowl and combine with flour and egg yolks.

2. Mix thoroughly by hand or in a mixer until your mixture forms a ball.

3. Let noodle dough rest for 8 hours.

4. If making noodles by hand, place dough onto a floured surface. Roll out very thin and cut into noodle shapes. If using a pasta machine, place dough onto a floured surface and roll out into a rectangle until it's approximately 1-inch thick. Cut into manageable rectangles to pass through your pasta machine. Start on the thickest setting and decrease setting size with each pass until desired thickness is reached.

© Amanda J. Paul

Pignolota

Located in Lambertville, New Jersey, near the Delaware River, Eight Hands Farm is a small family business made up of eight working hands. Apart from our handmade goods, we also have a seasonal honor system–style farm stand that offers fresh vegetables, cut flowers, and honey. These Sicilian Honey Balls, also known as Pignolota, have been a family tradition since I can remember. My grandma would ship them to us in a much-anticipated holiday tin every Christmas; by the time they arrived, the honey would be soaked into the dough perfectly. We are so excited to continue this tradition with our kids, using the honey from our farm.

Serves: 12 | Prep time: 20 minutes | Rest time: 2 hours | Cook time: 30 minutes

Ingredients

1 pound flour
4 large eggs (or as much as the flour takes)
1 tablespoon baking powder
Vegetable oil (for frying)
¼ cup sugar
1 tablespoon cinnamon
2 pounds honey
½ bottle rainbow nonpareils sprinkles

Instructions

1. In a bowl, combine flour, eggs and baking powder and mix.

2. Turn the dough out onto a lightly floured work surface and knead it until it is smooth. Cover the dough and let it rest for a couple of hours.

3. Divide the dough into 8 pieces and roll into ropes (about ½-inch thick). Cut ropes into pea-size pieces.

© Dena Greenwood

4. Heat oil in a large heavy saucepan to 350°F. Carefully add about 6 pieces of dough at a time and fry until they are evenly browned, about 3 minutes.

5. Remove the dough pieces with a slotted spoon and drain on a paper towel-lined plate. Repeat process until you fry all the pieces of dough.

© Dena Greenwood

6. In a large skillet, warm the sugar, cinnamon, and honey.

7. Add fried dough balls to the skillet and stir to coat them evenly with the honey. Cook for 5 minutes, until they obtain a glaze.

8. Immediately place them on serving plate, stacking them like a pinecone, and toss sprinkles on top.

© Jody D. White

Turkey, Wild Rice, and Pumpkin Soup

When our fiber farm, Wing & a Prayer Farm, first started, it was a hobby farm with a few chickens. Turkeys and ducks followed, and so on, and so on. For many years we have raised Heritage Breed Turkeys to sell for Thanksgiving in our community. Given their friendly nature, it is very easy to "pardon" our turkeys any time of the year. When we do raise them for the table, they are allowed to free-range their entire lives, a much longer duration than the commercial industry, which allows them to develop richer and healthier meat. The following is a delicious and hearty way to prepare some of your Thanksgiving leftovers.

Serves: 12 | Prep time: 20 minutes or longer if making turkey stock from scratch |
Cook time: 20 minutes

Ingredients

2 tablespoons butter or olive oil

½ cup chopped onions

½ cup sliced celery

1 teaspoon celery seed, or ¼ cup celeriac, minced

4 cups chicken or turkey broth

1 (16-ounce) can solid-pack pumpkin (I use my own roasted pumpkin)

2 cups cooked turkey, cubed (I use our smoked turkey!)

2 cups cooked wild rice

1 cup half-and-half

1 teaspoon seasoned salt

½ teaspoon ground cinnamon

Instructions

1. Cook and stir butter or olive oil, onions, and celery in Dutch oven over medium heat until vegetables are crisp-tender, about 5 minutes.

2. Add broth and pumpkin. Bring to a boil, then reduce heat and simmer for 5 minutes.

3. Stir in turkey, rice, half-and-half, salt, and cinnamon. Heat to serving temperature; do not boil.

4. Serve hot in a shallow bowl on a cold afternoon or evening with leftover Thanksgiving sandwiches or breads or just as is. Our family loves this soup with a slice of cranberry bread on the side!

Maple Cinnamon Rolls

North Road Sugarworks is a producer of pure, artisan maple syrup located at the foothills of the scenic Catskills Mountains of New York. Our first-generation maple farm is owned and operated by myself (Danielle Buck) and my husband Chase. Breakfast has long been the most important meal of the day for farmers. It's a chance to discuss our plan for the day, fuel up, and then put in a good day's work. These Maple Cinnamon Rolls are a favorite on our farm—they are simple to make and the ingredients are easy to come by. We hope you enjoy our sweet little spin on this classic breakfast treat!

Serves: 10–12 | Prep time: 1½ hours | Cook time: 25 minutes

Ingredients

Dough

2¾ cups all-purpose flour
¼ cup maple granulated
    sugar
½ teaspoon salt
1 packet instant yeast
½ cup whole milk
¼ cup water
2 tablespoons salted butter
1 large egg

Filling

½ cup maple granulated
    sugar
1 tablespoon cinnamon
1 tablespoon unsalted
    butter, softened

Icing

4 ounces cream cheese
2 tablespoons unsalted
    butter, softened
¾ cup confectioners' sugar
2 tablespoons maple syrup

Instructions

1. For the dough, in a large bowl whisk together flour, maple sugar, salt, and yeast.

2. In a small bowl, microwave milk, water, and butter together for 1½ minutes. Pour warm mixture into dry ingredients and stir or use dough hook attachment for electric mixer. Add egg and mix until a ball of soft dough forms, making sure not to overmix.

3. On a lightly floured surface knead dough for 2 to 3 minutes.

4. Place dough in a greased bowl and cover for 10 minutes. Make sure air can get in; a tight seal is not necessary.

5. For the filling, mix together the maple sugar and cinnamon.

6. After 10 minutes, roll the dough into a rectangle of approximately 12" × 8" on a lightly floured surface.

7. Spread softened butter on the dough, then sprinkle the filling mixture evenly across the surface.

8. Roll the dough tightly, then cut it into 12 even sections.

9. Place rolls in a lightly greased 9" × 9" pan, cover tightly with plastic wrap, and allow them

© Danielle Buck

to rise for 1 hour. They should double in size. If they do not double in size after 1 hour, allow them to rise for 30 more minutes.

10. While dough is rising, preheat oven to 375°F. Bake rolls for 25 minutes or until golden brown on top.

11. For the icing, beat together cream cheese, butter, confectioners' sugar, and maple syrup. Spread frosting over warm rolls and enjoy!

Traditional Potato Salad

We established Crooked Chimney Farm, a small hobby farm and homestead located on Maine's Mid-Coast, in 2018. We raise dairy goats, chickens, and ducks, along with our two trusty canine companions. We have a passion for making our own handcrafted goat milk soap and sharing our growing farm experiences with others. We chose to contribute this traditional dish because we wanted to share a recipe that not only has been passed down in the family, but also features one of Maine's most important and celebrated crops: the potato.

Serves: 8 | Prep time: 10 minutes | Total time: 25 minutes

Ingredients

5 potatoes, peeled
1½ cups mayonnaise
1 tablespoon yellow mustard
1 teaspoon celery salt
1 teaspoon celery seed
3 tablespoons sweet pickle juice
4 hardboiled eggs, peeled and chopped
2 stalks celery, diced
1 cup diced sweet pickles
Salt and pepper, to taste
Paprika and parsley, to garnish

Instructions

1. In a large pot, boil the potatoes in salted water until tender, about 15 minutes. Drain and let cool slightly. Cut the potatoes into 1-inch cubes.

2. In a large bowl, combine the mayonnaise, mustard, celery salt, celery seed, and pickle juice. Stir until well combined.

3. Fold in the potatoes, hardboiled eggs, celery, and pickles. Mix and season with salt and pepper.

4. Garnish with paprika and parsley, if desired.

5. Chill until ready to serve.

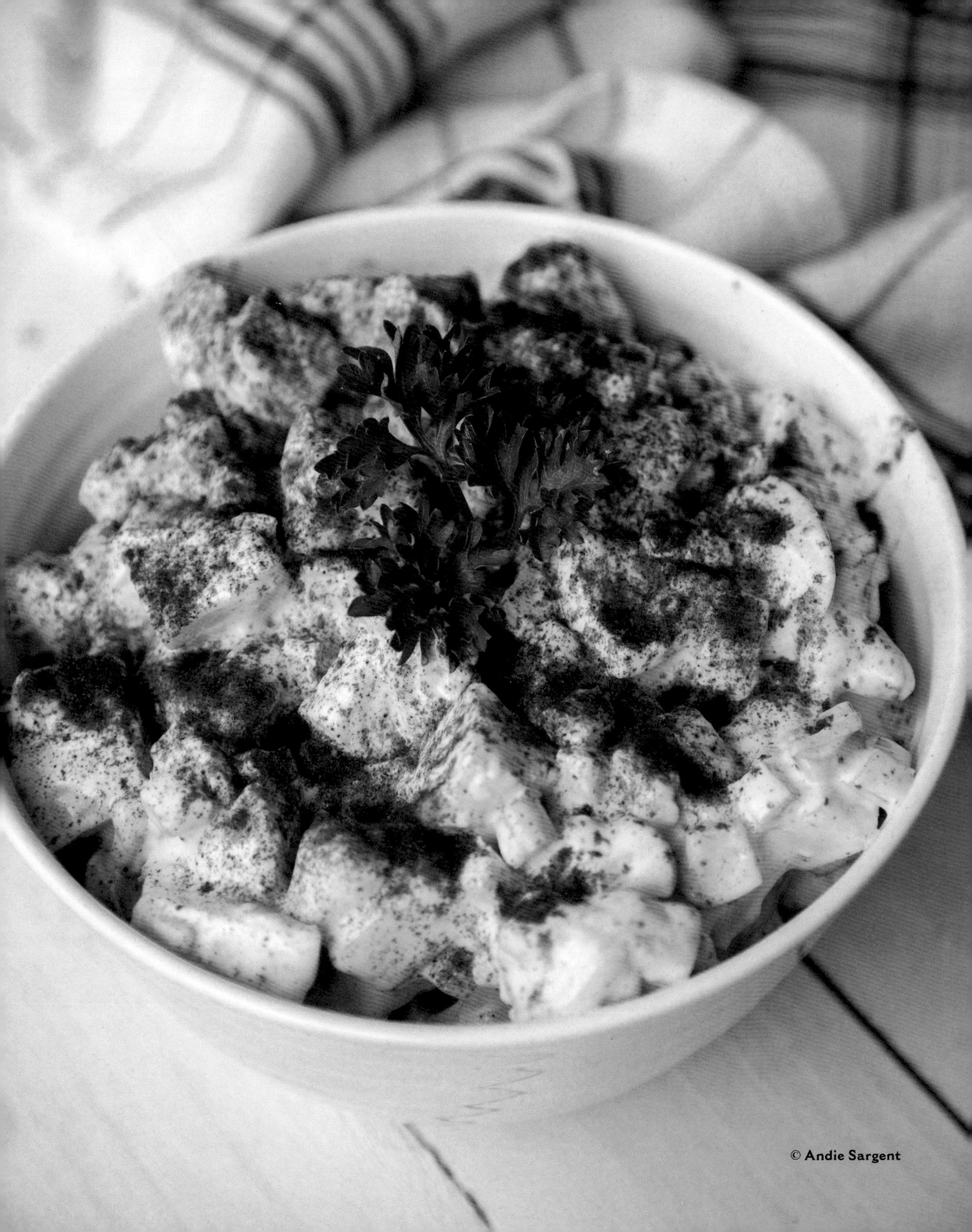

© Jenny McNulty @wyldephoto

Vernon Family Farm's Ramen

Vernon Family Farm is a pastured poultry farm, raising non-GMO pastured chicken. We have a complete list of chicken and value-added products that we make and sell at our on-site farm store. Highlighting ingredients grown and produced at our pastured livestock farm and sold at our farm store, this ramen recipe is super versatile and calls for the chef to make it their own, depending on what's in season and where they live. This dish is a staple in our home, showcasing ramen broth, chicken, and eggs, and produced and raised at our farm in Southern New Hampshire.

Serves: 4–6 people | Prep time: 30 minutes | Cook time: 45 minutes

Ingredients

2 tablespoons olive oil, divided
1 pound boneless skinless chicken
  breast
Salt, to taste
Pepper, to taste
Garlic powder, to taste
1 tablespoon butter
1 tablespoon sesame oil
2 cloves garlic, minced
2 teaspoons freshly grated ginger
½ cup diced onions

2 diced carrots
1 cup chopped shiitake, chestnut, or oyster
  mushrooms
1 tablespoon Sriracha sauce (exclude if you don't love
  heat!)
2 quarts Vernon Family Farm ramen broth*
6 ounces dried ramen noodles (rice noodles work
  great too!)
1 cup seasonal greens such as bok choy, tatsoi,
  spinach, swiss chard)
4–6 poached eggs (1 per person)

Instructions

1. Heat 1 tablespoon olive oil in a skillet over medium-high heat. Sprinkle each chicken breast with a pinch of salt, pepper, and garlic powder.

2. Once olive oil is hot, add the chicken breasts to the skillet. Brown chicken for 5 minutes on each side. Add butter to the skillet and cook until chicken breasts reach an internal temperature of 165°F. Cooking time will always depend on the thickness of the chicken breasts.

* Vernon Family Farm has an incredible variety of bone broths made with pastured chicken bones and feet available at our farm store, but if you don't live locally to the Seacoast of New Hampshire, we encourage you to make your own broth with pastured chickens from a farm near you. The secret to the ramen flavor is incorporating extra ingredients like gluten-free soy sauce, ginger, and lemongrass.

(continued on next page)

3. Transfer chicken breasts to a cutting board, let rest for 5 minutes, and slice. Cover sliced chicken breasts to keep warm.

4. Heat remaining olive oil and sesame oil in a large stockpot over moderate heat. Add garlic and ginger and simmer until fragrant, about 2 minutes. Add onions, carrots, and mushrooms and simmer until they soften, about 2 to 3 minutes, stirring occasionally.

5. Add ramen broth to the stockpot and add Sriracha sauce. Stir well to combine and bring broth to a simmer for about 5 minutes. Add more Sriracha if desired.

6. Add ramen noodles to stockpot and turn off heat (the heat from the soup will soften the noodles). Add seasonal greens to stockpot (the heat from the soup will also wilt the greens).

7. In a separate stove-top pot bring water to a gentle boil (small consistent bubbles and steam).

8. Crack each egg into a small bowl carefully. The trick to a beautifully formed poached egg is to keep the white as tight as possible.

9. Slowly pour the eggs into the gently boiling water and turn off heat.

10. Cook eggs for 4 minutes.

11. Ladle soup into bowls and top with cooked, sliced chicken breasts and 1 poached egg to each individual bowl. Enjoy!

Chai Elderberry Syrup

Welcome to our homestead! We are Brook and Sarah Stutzman. We are two crazy kids that fell in love with each other, started a garden, and a family. Well Folk Revival was born on a three-acre farm in Pennsylvania where we raise our children, grow our food, care for animals, practice functional medicine, and teach our community these ancestral roots through Folk School Classes and Health Coaching. Elderberry syrup is one of the ways we keep our children healthy during cold and flu season. We grow our own elderberries during summer and freeze them for recipes such as jams, syrup, and wine, but you can also source elderberries from farmers in your area, wild forage for them in nature, or pick them up at your local health food store. This recipe pulls together the benefits of elderberry and many spices known to have antiviral and antibacterial benefits.

© Sarah Stutzman

Serves: 16 | Prep time: 5 minutes | Cook time: 1 hour

Ingredients

3½ cups water

⅔ cup dried black elderberries or 1⅓ cups fresh or frozen black elderberries

2 tablespoons sliced ginger

1–2 cinnamon sticks

3 cardamom pods, crushed (use a mortar and pestle)

4 clove buds

5 peppercorns

1 anise star

1 cup raw honey

Instructions

1. Pour water into a medium saucepan and add the elderberries and spices. Bring to a boil, then reduce to a simmer for about 45 minutes to 1 hour until the liquid has reduced by almost half.

2. Remove from heat and let cool until it is lukewarm or cool enough to handle.

3. Mash the berries carefully using a spoon or other flat utensil. Pour through a strainer into a bowl.

4. Discard the elderberries and let the liquid cool to room temperature. When it is no longer hot, add the honey. Stir well.

5. When the honey is well-mixed into the elderberry mixture, pour the syrup into a quart mason jar or 16-ounce glass bottle of any kind. Ta-da, you just made homemade elderberry syrup! Store in the refrigerator and take 1 tablespoon for adults and 1 teaspoon for children daily for its immune boosting properties. Increase as needed when you feel sick. The finished syrup will last in the refrigerator for up to 2 weeks. Pro tip: If taken only by adults, add ½ cup brandy to the syrup to increase preservation for up to 1 month. You can use less honey if you use this method.

Homemade Sweet and Sour Pickles

Silverwood Organic Farm is situated on over one hundred acres of owned and leased land in Sherborn, Massachusetts, a small town in the western suburbs of Boston. Silverwood Organic Farm's mission is to reclaim and restore historic farmland as a community resource for the production of certified organic, locally grown produce using sustainable farming methods. These pickles are a staple in our household during the summer when we have mass amounts of cucumbers. They pair perfectly with burgers, sandwiches, and salads, but we often end up eating them straight from the jar! These pickles also last in your fridge for many weeks, so you can enjoy them for as long as you want.

Serves: 1 quart jar pickles | Prep time: 20 minutes | Processing time: 48 hours

Ingredients
2 medium cucumbers

1 medium white onion, thinly sliced

½ cup white vinegar

½ cup water

5 tablespoons sugar

½ teaspoon salt

Instructions
1. Wash cucumbers and leave peel on.

2. Use a fork to scrape deep stripes the length of the cucumber on all sides.

3. Cut cucumber into thin slices.

4. Place cucumber and onion slices into a large jar with a lid.

5. In a small bowl, mix together vinegar, water, sugar, and salt until the sugar and salt are completely dissolved.

6. Pour brine into jar to cover the cucumbers and onions.

7. Cover jar tightly and refrigerate.

8. Pickles will be ready to eat in 48 hours and will keep (refrigerated) for several weeks.

© Blake Hill Preserves

Triple Jalapeño Poppers

Blake Hill Preserves is a fruit preservatory in Vermont creating innovative sweet, savory, and spicy jams, marmalades, and condiments for the modern pantry. My husband Joe grew up in Gibraltar—a British colony on the tip of the Iberian Peninsula—with a Spanish, North African, and Italian cooking heritage, and a natural intuition for the best uses for a wide range of spices. We celebrate this passion in a full line of spicy chili jams made from farm-fresh Vermont chili peppers. The perfect amount of sweetness balances the heat of this jam in our favorite appetizer, poppers!

Serves: 24 poppers | Prep time: 10 minutes | Cook time: 15 minutes

Ingredients

8 ounces cream cheese at room temperature

4 tablespoons Blake Hill's Jalapeño & Lime Spicy Chili Jam* or other jam of choice

12 jalapeño peppers

Instructions

1. Preheat oven to 350°F. Line a sheet tray with parchment paper and set aside.

2. Combine cream cheese with jam (reserving 2 tablespoons) in a bowl.

3. Slice jalapeño peppers in half lengthwise, deseed, and stuff with the spicy jalapeño cream cheese.

4. Place poppers on the parchment-lined sheet tray and bake for 15 minutes.

5. Drizzle reserved jam over poppers and enjoy!

*Purchase here: https://blakehillpreserves.com/products/jalapeno-lime-spicy-chili-jam?_pos=3&_sid=7be562dl6&_ss=r)

Garden Vegetable and Oyster Mushroom Pizza

Candlewood Valley Mushrooms is an organic, gourmet, and medicinal mushroom farm in Western Connecticut. We pride ourselves on cultivating uncommon varieties of gourmet mushrooms such as oyster, chestnut, maitake, and lion's mane. This recipe's mix of savory sauteed oyster mushrooms and fresh garden vegetables makes for a truly enchanting pizza experience.

Serves: 8 | Prep time: 1½ hours | Cook time: 8–10 minutes

Ingredients

Dough

1 (¼-ounce) packet active dry yeast
1 cup warm water (between 100–110°F)
2 cups all-purpose flour, divided
1 tablespoon granulated sugar
1 teaspoon kosher salt
1 teaspoon garlic powder
1 tablespoon dried basil
2 tablespoons olive oil
Sprinkle of cornmeal, for dusting the pan

Mushrooms and Sauce

3 tablespoons butter, divided
4–6 ounces fresh oyster mushrooms, sliced
1 tablespoon olive oil

¼ cup finely chopped onion
2 cloves or 1 large clove garlic, minced
3 tablespoons all-purpose flour
1 cup milk, plus more as needed
½ cup grated Parmesan cheese
2 tablespoons minced fresh basil
½ teaspoon chopped fresh oregano
¼ teaspoon salt
⅛ teaspoon ground black pepper

Toppings

Sautéed oyster mushrooms
Fresh tomato slices
Fresh pepper slices
6–8 ounces shredded mozzarella

Instructions

1. For the dough, mix yeast and warm water in the bowl of your stand mixer. (If you don't have a stand mixer, simply use a large mixing bowl and mix the dough by hand with a wooden spoon.) Wait 15 minutes to activate the yeast, then add 1 cup flour and the remaining dry ingredients to the bowl. Whisk by hand until smooth. Place the bowl in your mixer on low speed with a dough hook. Add the rest of the flour gradually until it forms a ball.

2. Lightly grease a large bowl with olive oil. Place the dough in the bowl, turning it to coat all sides in the oil. Cover the bowl with plastic wrap and put it in a warm place to rise for 30 minutes. It should double in size.

© Kimberly Gaeta

3. Sprinkle a baking sheet or pizza pan with cornmeal. When the dough is ready, knead it on a floured surface to release any air bubbles. Gently flatten the dough, place on the prepared pan, and stretch it to fit. Let the dough rest and rise again in the pan for 30 minutes.

4. For the mushrooms and sauce, heat 1 tablespoon butter in a medium saucepan over medium heat. Add mushrooms and sauté until golden brown, then remove mushrooms from the pan and set aside.

5. Using the same pan, add the remaining butter and olive oil. Add the onion and garlic and cook until tender and fragrant, about 1 minute. Add flour and whisk until flour is lightly browned and onion is translucent, 2 to 3 minutes.

6. Mix milk, Parmesan cheese, basil, oregano, salt, and black pepper into the onion mixture. Cook, whisking continuously, until cheese has melted, and sauce has thickened slightly, about 5 minutes. Remove from heat.

7. Preheat the oven to 450°F. Prebake the dough for 1 minute before adding toppings. Remove from the oven, add sauce, and toppings. Return to the oven and bake for 8 to 10 more minutes or until the crust is golden and the cheese is bubbly. Slice and serve immediately.

© Beth Falk, Home To Roost

Great Grandma's Blueberry Buckle

I am Beth, @hometoroost on Instagram, and our small farm is nestled on a dead-end road in rural Western New York. We raise our own beef, pork, chicken, eggs, and grow a large vegetable garden, from which we preserve foods to carry us through much of the year. When I was a kid, I remember going to my great grandparents' house in the summer. They had rows upon rows of blueberry bushes. I have no idea how many, but as a kid, it felt like a million. My grandmother would create a makeshift bucket out of an old milk jug and tie it to our waists for easy picking (or one hand for picking, one hand for eating). We'd pick gallons and gallons of berries for the freezer, but during blueberry season there was always fresh buckle. This is my great grandmother's recipe and I hope you enjoy it as much as we do.

Serves: 10 | Prep time: 15 minutes | Cook time: 50–55 minutes

Ingredients

¼ cup butter

½ cup sugar

1 farm-fresh egg, well beaten

1 cup flour

1½ teaspoons baking powder

⅛ teaspoon salt

⅓ cup milk

1 teaspoon vanilla

2 cups blueberries

Topping

½ cup sugar

¼ cup butter

⅓ cup flour

½ teaspoon cinnamon

Instructions

1. Preheat oven to 375°F.

2. Cream butter, sugar, and egg.

3. In a separate bowl mix dry ingredients together.

4. Add dry ingredients to the creamed mixture, alternating with milk and vanilla.

5. For topping, combine all topping ingredients.

6. Pour batter into a well-greased cast-iron skillet, cover with berries, then sprinkle with topping.

7. Bake for 50 to 55 minutes. Check middle of buckle with a toothpick to ensure it's done.

© Chris Bassette

Chocolate Zucchini Cake

Killam & Bassette Farmstead is a family-run farm that has been in business since 1893 with a long tradition of hard work and pride in all that we do. Our five children and eighty-nine-year-old partner help us run our family farm and produce quality meats, eggs, award-winning canned goods, and more. We harvest over eighty-eight acres of Connecticut River Valley land and are very honored to be a part of our New England farming community. This recipe is a farm and customer favorite.

Serves: 8–12 | Prep time: 25 minutes | Cook time: 1 hour

Ingredients

2½ cups flour

5 tablespoons cocoa

1½ teaspoons baking powder

1½ teaspoons baking soda

1 teaspoon cinnamon

½ cup milk

3 eggs

¾ cup butter, softened

2 cups sugar

2 teaspoons vanilla

2 cups zucchini

Instructions

1. Preheat oven to 350°F.

2. Stir all dry ingredients together except sugar.

3. Cream eggs, butter, sugar, and vanilla together.

4. Stir dry ingredients into creamed ingredients and mix well.

5. Add zucchini and mix well.

6. Pour into a large, greased tube pan and bake for 1 hour.

7. Test cake with a toothpick to ensure it's done, then turn off heat and leave in the oven for a few minutes. Cake is delicious plain or may be glazed, frosted, or sprinkled with confectioners' sugar. It also freezes well.

© Alison Sacks

Cola-Braised Pork Shoulder with Chipotle Adobo Sauce

I am a wife, mother, maker, and bread baker. My husband and I founded Catoctin Mountain Farm where we proudly raise heritage pork in the Catoctin Mountains of Northern Maryland. This is the first dish I created as a newly wedded farm wife and I've made it a tradition to serve it to many visitors of the farm. The cola braises the meat to tender fall-off-the-bone perfection with a touch of sweetness and the chipotle adobo sauce adds a kick of heat and tang. Serve with classic taco toppings or rice and beans for a new family favorite.

Serves: 6 | Prep time: 15 minutes | Cook time: 8 hours

Ingredients

3 tablespoons brown sugar
3 tablespoons paprika
2 tablespoons kosher salt
2 teaspoons pepper
2 teaspoons garlic powder
2 teaspoons onion powder
2 teaspoons dried oregano
½ teaspoon cayenne pepper
3–4 pounds pork shoulder
2 yellow onions, quartered
5 cups cola (Coke, Dr. Pepper, Root Beer)
½ cup mayonnaise
4 tablespoons lemon juice
3–4 chipotle peppers in adobo sauce
1–2 cloves garlic, minced
¼ teaspoon kosher salt

Instructions

1. In a small bowl, mix brown sugar, paprika, salt, pepper, garlic powder, onion powder, oregano, and cayenne pepper together in a bowl. Coat pork shoulder well with this rub on all sides. Place in a slow cooker, add onions and cola, and cook on low for 8 hours.

2. For the sauce, add the mayonnaise, lemon juice, chipotle peppers, garlic, and salt to a food processor or blender. Blend until smooth. Refrigerate until serving.

3. After the pork is done, place it on a plate and pull it apart with two forks. Serve with classic taco toppings or rice and beans and the chipotle adobo sauce.

Deep South Region

Grain-Free Italian Stuffed Peppers

I'm Kathleen Henderson, the natural living mentor behind the Roots & Boots *blog and YouTube channel, and the creator of the brand-new Real Food Family Meal Plan, saving time and money in kitchens across the country. My family grows real food on a twenty-acre farm in Northern Virginia. My husband, three sons, and I raise pastured eggs, pastured meats, and fresh vegetables. We offer our beyond-organic meats to the local community via CSA meat shares. One of my very favorite things is to sit down with my family to a 100 percent homegrown meal, like these Grain-Free Italian Stuffed Peppers. Remember: stuffed pepper recipes, including this one, are more of a loose guide than a strict recipe. Feel free to substitute other meats or no meat at all, as well as alternative vegetables. If you're a garlic fan, go ahead and increase the number of cloves.*

Serves: 8 | Prep time: 15 minutes | Cook time: 1 hour

Ingredients

8 medium bell peppers

1 teaspoon unrefined sea salt, plus more as needed

Pepper, to taste

2 tablespoons oil

1 medium onion, diced

3 cloves garlic, minced

1 pound ground beef (grass-fed is best)

1 tablespoon Italian seasoning (or ½ heaping teaspoon each of rosemary, basil, parsley, oregano, and thyme)

1½ cups riced cauliflower, cooked

1 (15-ounce) can diced tomatoes, drained, or 1–2 cups chopped fresh tomatoes

1 cup shredded raw cheddar cheese

Optional: thinly sliced scallions, to garnish

Instructions

1. Preheat oven to 375°F.

2. Remove the top of each pepper (dice tops and reserve for adding to the filling) and discard seeds and membranes.

3. Place the peppers in a baking dish and season inside with salt and pepper.

4. In a large pan, heat the oil over medium heat. When hot, add onion and cook until softened. Then, add in the diced pepper tops and cook briefly. Next, add in the garlic and cook for about 1 minute, until fragrant.

5. Add in the ground beef and cook until brown. When the beef is almost browned, add the Italian seasoning and stir well to combine.

6. When the beef is browned, remove from heat, and stir in riced cauliflower and tomatoes. Season as needed with salt and pepper.

7. Divide the mixture evenly between the peppers.

8. Top each pepper with shredded cheddar.

9. Add 1 cup water to the baking dish, carefully pouring it between the peppers.

10. Grease one side of a large sheet of tin foil and place this side down on top of the peppers. Cover tightly, securing all four sides to the baking dish.

11. Bake for 1 hour, until the peppers are softened, but not mushy. The filling should be heated through. If you want to get fancy, thinly slice the green part of a green onion or two, and sprinkle on top of each pepper before serving.

© Kathleen Henderson

© Emily Taylorson

Gourmet Pickled Eggs

We are accidental homesteaders, making our way on Two Acre Farm. With gardening and chickens eventually came the need to learn preserving. Once we figured out canning, playing around with the idea of pickled eggs was fun! We've created several flavors and like to call them "gourmet" pickled eggs. These are our original recipes.

Cajun Pickled Eggs

Serves: 2 quart jars | Prep time: 10 minutes | Cook time: 25 minutes

Ingredients
50/50 white vinegar and water
12 boiled eggs, peeled
2 tablespoons powdered crab boil
2–3 teaspoon red pepper flakes

Instructions
1. Bring 50/50 white vinegar and water to a boil.
2. Divide eggs between 2 quart jars with lids and add seasonings.
3. Pour boiling hot brine over eggs until covered.
4. Wipe the jar rims dry and place lids on top.
5. Let completely cool on the counter. Once cool, place in the refrigerator. You can eat these pickled eggs immediately, but it's recommended to wait at least 1 week. The longer they sit, the more flavor they will have.

© Emily Taylorson

Garlic Dill Pickled Eggs

Serves: 2 quart jars | Prep time: 10 minutes | Cook time: 25 minutes

Ingredients

4¼ cups water

2⅛ cups white vinegar

¼ cup salt (we use canning salt)

10–12 boiled eggs, peeled

3 teaspoons dried dill weed or fresh dill (if using fresh dill, add as much as you want)

8 cloves freshly peeled garlic

¼ cup very thinly sliced onion

¾ cup very thinly sliced jalapeño

2–4 teaspoons red pepper flakes or cayenne pepper

Instructions

1. Bring water, white vinegar, and salt to a boil.

2. Divide eggs between 2 quart jars and add seasoning.

3. Pour boiling hot brine over eggs until covered.

4. Wipe the jar rims dry and place lids on top.

5. Let completely cool on the counter. Once cool, place in the refrigerator. You can eat these pickled eggs immediately, but it's recommended to wait at least 1 week. The longer they sit, the more flavor they will have.

© Emily Taylorson

Chicken Pot Pie

I own and run Bingham Farm with my husband and three free-range farm kids in the beautiful piedmont of North Carolina. Our goal is for our farm to be a place for the community to come learn about farming as well as enjoy a fresh farm-to-table meal made by us (farmers) in the upcoming year. Having completely revived a one-hundred-year-old farmhouse and old family homestead to grow organic vegetables and pastured meats, we present a traditional southern dish chock-full of all the wonderful things our farm provides.

Serving: 8 | Prep time: 30 minutes | Cook time: 30 minutes

Ingredients

Pie Crust
2½ cups all-purpose flour, plus more as needed
½ tablespoon granulated sugar
½ teaspoon sea salt
½ pound cold butter, diced into ¼-inch pieces
7 tablespoons cold water
1 egg, beaten (egg wash)

Pie Filling
6 tablespoons butter
1 medium yellow onion, diced
2 medium stalks celery, diced

1 large carrot, diced
2.5 ounces sliced mushrooms
3 fresh cloves garlic, minced
⅓ cup all-purpose flour
2 cups chicken stock
½ cup heavy whipping cream
Sea salt and pepper, to taste
½ teaspoon dried thyme
½ teaspoon Redmond Season Salt
3 cups cooked chicken
½ cup green peas
1 cup green beans
½ cup sweet corn

Instructions

1. For the pie crust, place flour, sugar, and salt into a large food processor and pulse it a few times to combine. Then, add in cold, diced butter and pulse until coarse crumbs form. Small pea-sized pieces are okay. Then, add cold water and pulse until the dough starts forming.

2. Transfer dough to a clean work surface that is sprinkled with flour. Gather dough into a ball. Do not knead. Divide the dough into two equal parts. Flatten both to form 2 (4–5 inches wide) disks, cover each with plastic wrap, and refrigerate for approximately 1 hour before using.

(continued on page 139)

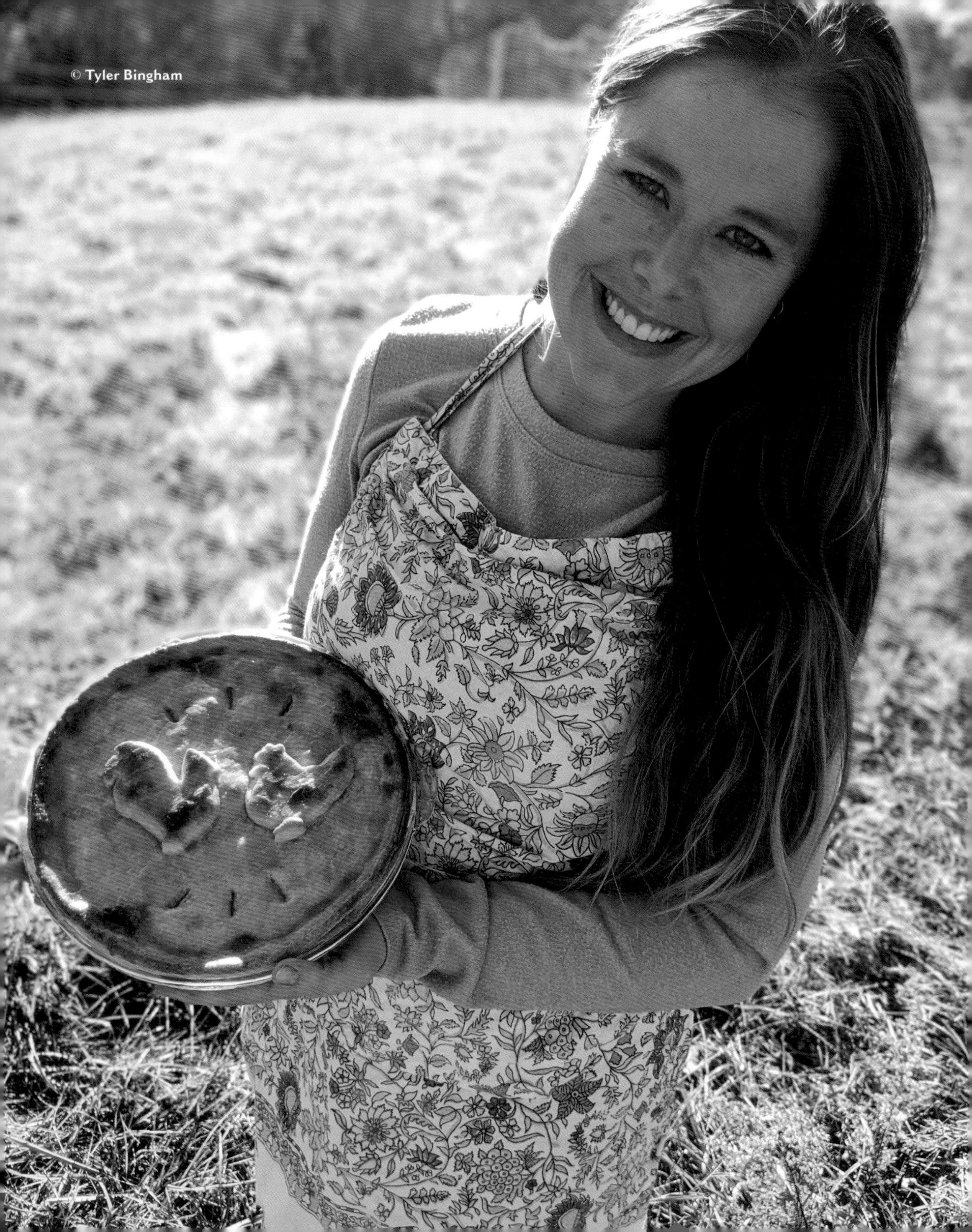

3. While your crusts are chilling in the fridge, make the pie filling. In a Dutch oven or large sauté pan, add butter. Add in onion, celery, and carrot and sauté over medium heat until soft, about 6 to 8 minutes. Then, add in mushrooms and garlic and sauté another 2 to 3 minutes until mushrooms are soft. Sprinkle in flour and stir constantly for 2 minutes. Add chicken stock and heavy cream. Bring to a simmer on medium-high heat and cook for 1 minute or until the mixture is thick like gravy. Season with sea salt, pepper, dried thyme, and season salt. Add in cooked chicken, peas, green beans, and corn.

4. Reduce heat to very low and let it simmer to keep warm while you assemble your pie crust in your pan. Remove pie crusts from fridge. Make sure they have been chilling for approximately 1 hour. Preheat your oven to 425°F. Roll 1 chilled pie crust into a 12-inch-wide circle. Carefully transfer it to a 9" × 9" pie pan and gently form it to the shape of the pan.

© Tyler Bingham

5. Spoon the pie filling over the bottom crust. Roll the second disk of pie dough into a 10-inch-wide circle and place it over the pie filling. Fold and cut any extra crust as desired. Crimp the pie crusts together to form a seal for your pie. Use a sharp knife and cut 6 small slits in your pie to allow steam to escape.

6. Brush the top of the crust with a beaten egg. Add any decorations to the crust as desired and apply a final egg wash to the entire pie. Do not allow egg wash to pool.

7. Bake for 30 to 35 minutes or until the top crust is golden brown. If the edges are browning too fast, place a layer of aluminum foil over the pie. Once out of the oven, let the pie rest for 15 minutes to cool before cutting.

Mexican Farm Frittata

There is something so satisfying about walking out your backdoor and grabbing ingredients straight from the garden for a homemade meal. Teaching our children how to grow and raise our own food is the goal here at Pine Valley Acres. Our chickens keep us supplied with eggs and our garden with the crisp, fresh vegetables needed to make this deliciously simple recipe. The best part about a frittata is that you can substitute or omit many of the ingredients to suit your taste and it comes out great every time. It really is a no-fail meal that is healthy and easy to prepare . . . a favorite on our farm!

Serves: 6 | Prep time: 15 minutes | Cook time: 20–25 minutes

Ingredients

2 tablespoons oil
1 bell pepper, diced
1 tomato, diced
1 onion, diced
8 ounces whole Baby Bella mushrooms, diced
1 tablespoon taco seasoning
8 eggs
Salt and pepper, to taste
1 cup shredded cheddar cheese
Optional: sour cream and scallions, to garnish

Instructions

1. Preheat oven to 400°F.

2. Heat a medium-sized skillet with oil to medium-high.

3. Sauté pepper, tomato, onion, and mushrooms in skillet until tender, about 10 minutes.

4. Stir taco seasoning into sautéed vegetables.

5. Whisk eggs in a bowl and add salt and pepper to taste.

6. Pour sautéed vegetables in a lightly greased pie pan or baking dish.

7. Pour in whisked eggs and cheese on top of vegetables and stir lightly to combine.

8. Bake for 20 to 25 minutes until center is firm and no longer runny.

9. Add a dollop of sour cream or slice scallions thinly and sprinkle on top before serving if you'd like.

© Shanna Mason

© Shanna Mason

Beef Bone Broth

My husband Buddy, our three farm boys, and I raise grass-fed and finished meats on our family farm, Capon Crossing Farm, in the mountains of West Virginia. I love sharing healthy farm food with others because it has helped me so much! Grass-fed bone broth is a whole food unto itself, filled with minerals, protein, healthy fats, and collagen. It has so many health benefits, and truly is a superfood. It is so handy to have on hand for soups, stews, and enriching recipes, and is easy to freeze.

Serves: 4½ quarts | Prep time: 15 minutes | Cook time: 24–48 hours

Ingredients
2–3 beef marrow bones
2 large carrots, chopped in half
2 celery stalks, chopped in half
1 onion, chopped in half
8 cloves garlic, peeled
1½ cups parsley
3 tablespoons sea salt
½ teaspoons black pepper
1¼ gallons (20 cups) water
2 tablespoons raw apple cider vinegar

Instructions
1. Place beef marrow bones along with the prepared vegetables and parsley in an 8-quart pot.

2. Add in sea salt and black pepper.

3. Pour water into pot over the beef marrow bones and vegetables.

4. Splash in raw apple cider vinegar.

5. Bring all to a boil, then turn down and bring to a simmer.

6. Allow to simmer on low for 24 to 48 hours.

7. Enjoy as a warm drink or use for cooking.

© Pat Riesenburger Schertz, a.k.a. "Mrs. Farmer"

Rosie Belle Farm's Almond Dill Crackers

We are a highly diversified small farm, raising sheep, goats, cows, chickens, and ducks. There are usually 3 to 5 Jersey cows in milk at any given time, which means that we get 7 to 12 gallons of milk every single day! We are proud of the cheese produced at Rosie Belle Farm and wanted to create a cracker that would complement our cheeses. These beautiful crackers are on point! We use fresh farm butter, farm eggs, and rich Jersey cow farm milk to create a cracker that is crispy, flaky, buttery, and delicious! They pair perfectly with a mild baby manchego or creamy ricotta.

Serves: 1 pound

Ingredients

1 cup bread flour, plus
  more as needed
¾ cup cake flour
2 teaspoons coarse kosher
  salt
2 teaspoons sugar
1 teaspoon baking powder
¼ pound butter, melted,
  plus more as needed
1 egg
6 tablespoons cold milk
Egg wash (1 egg white
  mixed with 2 tablespoons
  water)
½ ounce fresh dill, chopped
¾ cup sliced raw almonds
Coarse kosher salt, to taste

Instructions

1. Preheat oven to 400°F.

2. Put flours, salt, sugar, baking powder, butter, egg, and milk into a mixing bowl and beat until well combined. Dough should be soft and pliable.

3. Dust work surface liberally with flour and place half the dough on the work surface (save the other half of the dough to make a second batch of crackers). Using a rolling pin, roll dough to ¼-inch thickness. Carefully flip dough over and roll to ⅛-inch thickness.

4. Use a pastry brush to liberally coat the dough with egg wash, which will enable the dill and almonds to adhere to the cracker.

5. Sprinkle chopped dill on the surface of the dough.

6. Sprinkle raw almonds on the surface of the dough, pressing them down slightly with the palm of your hand.

7. Dust the surface of the dough with a sprinkle of kosher salt.

8. Cut the dough horizontally and vertically to create individual crackers, then place them on a parchment-lined cookie sheet.

9. Bake for 8 minutes, rotate pan, and bake for an additional 4 to 6 minutes until crackers are golden with light brown edges.

10. Brush the tops of the crackers with melted butter.

11. Let the crackers cool completely before eating as they will continue to "crisp up" as they cool. Note: Air is the enemy to a crisp cracker! They will keep in a covered container in the pantry for 1 week or more. They also freeze beautifully—just pop them in the oven for a moment if they need to crisp up.

© Alysha Sneed

Granny's Giblet Gravy

We are a family of six living on a small seven acres near the Arkansas/Oklahoma border called Sneed Acres. We have chickens that lay a rainbow of egg colors, goats that we milk for soap, and we have been raising sheep for a couple of years for meat and wool. Thanksgiving and Christmas are not complete in our family without this gravy. Granny was making it for at least forty-five years before my mom and aunts took over, but we think her mom made it this way before her. We have several different versions now because my mom prefers chicken thighs and chicken stock to giblets and drippings and one of my aunts prefers chicken breast. My mom also uses cornstarch, but my granny used flour. So, feel free to make it your own!

Serves: 8 | Prep time: 10 minutes | Cook time: 15 minutes

Ingredients

3 cups chicken or giblet broth

¼ cup butter

¼ teaspoon salt, plus more to taste

⅛ teaspoon pepper or more to taste

Cooked giblet meat or some cooked dark meat from your bird, diced

1 cup drippings

2 boiled eggs, peeled and diced

4 tablespoons all-purpose flour

6–8 tablespoons water

Instructions

1. If using chicken broth, when your chicken is just finished and resting, combine broth, butter, salt, pepper, dark meat, drippings, and eggs in a medium pot. If using giblet broth, simmer your giblet broth for a couple of hours, then strain it, cut the useable meat off the neck, and finely chop the remaining organs. If you don't like the taste of liver, remove it before making the broth.

2. In a small cup or jar, combine flour with 6 tablespoons water. If the mixture is pasty and thick, add 1 to 2 more tablespoons of water. Pour flour mixture into the gravy while stirring continually and let simmer for a couple of minutes to thicken.

3. Serve while still hot!

© Kiona & Chris Wagner, Rocky Soil Family Farm

Braised Pork Belly in Vanilla-Bourbon Glaze

As first-generation farmers, we quit our jobs and relocated to Monticello, Florida, in 2019 to open Rocky Soil Family Farm. Our interest in growing food started with a small garden that soon became our backyard oasis which fed neighbors and colleagues daily. We now have thirteen acres of land to grow vegetables, raise chickens for fresh eggs, and host farm-to-table dinners. This recipe is our idea of elevated comfort food and can be plated for a high-end dinner or a fun family backyard gathering.

Serves: 4 | Prep time: 30–45 minutes | Cook time: 3–4 hours

Ingredients

Pork Belly
1 (4-pound) pre-cured pork belly, skin on
2 pounds pure salt
1½ grams sodium nitrate (optional)
1 cup bourbon
⅓ vanilla bean, scraped
1 pound brown sugar

Braising Liquid
2 cups water
1 cup bourbon
⅓ vanilla bean, scraped
1 cup sugarcane syrup
1 onion, chopped
5 whole cloves garlic
1 carrot, diced
10 peppercorns

Vanilla-Bourbon Glaze
⅓ vanilla bean, scraped
¼ cup bourbon
1 cup sugarcane syrup
¼ cup brown sugar
½ lemon juice

Instructions

1. Preheat oven to 375°F.

2. Marinate pre-cured pork belly in pork belly ingredients. Remove cured belly out of salt brine and wash off. Dry off pork belly and score the skin diagonally in both directions.

3. Combine braising liquid ingredients.

4. In a skillet, sear pork belly, then add braising liquid and braise in the oven until tender.

5. Combine vanilla-bourbon glaze ingredients.

6. Remove pork belly from liquid and place on a baking sheet.

7. Add glaze to pork belly and return to oven to bake. Repeat several times until the glaze is gone.

8. Serve hot over pureed parsnips with roasted carrots or your favorite veggies.

Wild Tea

Herb Mountain Farm, located in Western North Carolina, has been growing vegetables and flowers organically since 1970. We host events at our beloved plant and healing sanctuary and rent it as an outdoor venue that accesses trails, gardens, fire circles, and ponds. We are a residential farm of twenty-five folks, all committed to stewarding our precious planet with care. Drinking locally is a passion of ours! We have been hosting Appalachian Tea Ceremonies at our farm to experience the different qualities of plants grown in our region. Give your plant friends a try!

Serves: 1 quart tea | Prep time: 5 minutes | Steep time: 10–20 minutes

Ingredients

1 quart water, plus more as needed

2 cups fresh or ½ cup dried leaves, seeds, flowers, and/or twigs of familiar, safe plants (There is no "exact" amount. The more you use, the stronger the tea will be. Dried material is stronger than fresh.)

Sweetener (optional)

Instructions

1. Harvest plants from your home or a nearby area that are safe to make into tea. Start with some better-known plants like leaves of violet or dandelion roots or mint. Some of our favorites are rose with nettle and red clover with sweet birch twigs.

2. Bring water to a boil in a non-aluminum covered half-gallon pot.

3. Take pot off heat, place plant material into the pot, and cover immediately to retain volatile oils for flavor. Let steep for twenty minutes.

© Mary Plantwalker

4. Strain plant material out of liquid with colander or tea strainer. If you have chickens, they love this compost!

5. Add sweetener if desired.

6. Pour yourself and a friend or family member a cup and enjoy!

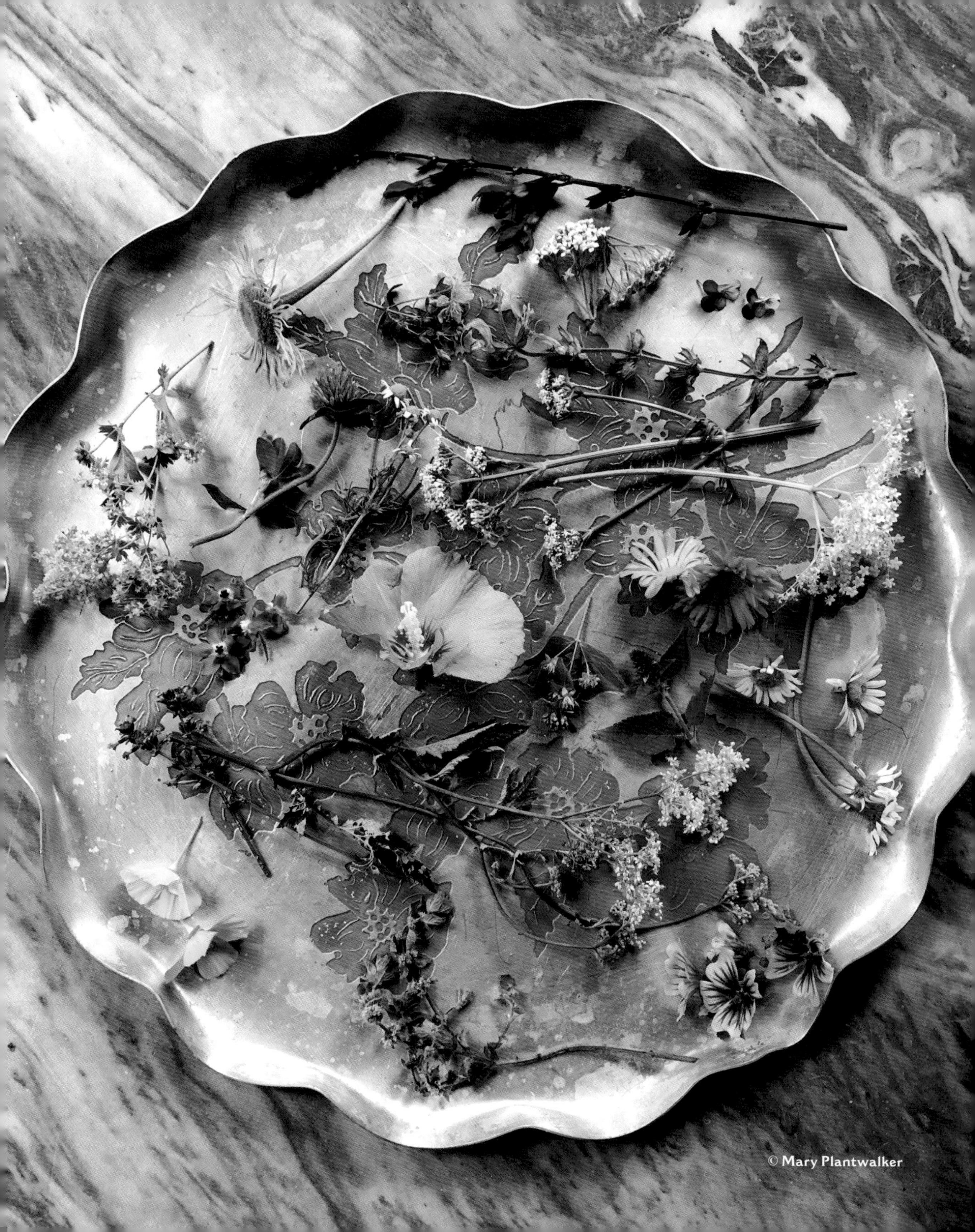

© Fawn Shear

Cinnamon-Maple Sourdough Bread

Seasons' Yield Farm and Bakery was a dream that began while stationed along the Arghandab River of Afghanistan on a deployment many years ago. Our family has since opened a wood-fired bakery on our eight-acre homestead in Raphine, Virginia. This Cinnamon-Maple Sourdough Bread is our signature loaf representing the best of the land and serving as a symbol of this new season of life for our family.

Serves: 1 loaf | Prep time: 7½ hours | Bake time: 45 minutes

Ingredients

12 ounces lukewarm water
3½ ounces Simple Sourdough Starter (recipe on page 80)
5 ounces whole wheat flour
13 ounces white flour
2 teaspoons salt
2 ounces maple syrup
2 teaspoons cinnamon
3 ounces seedless raisins

Instructions

1. Gently mix together the water and sourdough starter. To this liquid mix, add both flours. Mix with your hand until the flour is hydrated and a loose dough has formed. Cover dough with plastic wrap or a towel and let stand for 1 hour at room temperature.

2. Add salt, syrup, cinnamon, and raisins to the dough. Squeeze and fold until mixed. Cover and let sit for 45 minutes.

3. Fold dough on top of itself 4 times. Cover and let sit for 45 minutes. Repeat this step until the dough has doubled in size, about 3 hours.

4. Turn the dough onto a work surface and shape into a round ball. Let sit for 15 minutes.

5. For the final shaping, form a boule by folding the corners of the dough into the middle. Then, flip the dough seam-side down onto your work surface and push and pull until a smooth ball is formed. Flip the dough seam-side up into a towel-lined bowl (or a Banneton proofing basket). Let rise for 3 or 4 hours until the dough does not spring back when lightly touched. For baking the next morning, place in the refrigerator.

6. One hour before baking, preheat the oven to 500°F. Place a Dutch oven (with lid on) inside oven to preheat as well. Let it preheat for 45 minutes. When preheated, remove Dutch oven and turn dough from the bowl into it. Score the loaf with scissors or a bread lame with deep cuts.

7. Turn down heat to 450°F and bake for 20 minutes, covered. Remove lid and bake for an additional 25 minutes. Remove the Dutch oven from the oven, remove the bread, and let bread cool completely on a rack or upended on the counter before slicing. This bread keeps well on the counter for up to 2 days, cut-side down, or covered loosely with plastic wrap in a bread box. This bread also freezes well.

Buttermilk Fried Chicken

I live on a cattle farm in Lancaster, Kentucky, and am the creator of the southern food blog Feast and Farm. *My husband and I were both raised on cattle and Burley tobacco farms, and enjoy tending black Angus cattle, organic produce, herbal remedies, and happy children in a slow lifestyle. My culinary emphasis is on creating recipes that use fewer processed ingredients. That's why this recipe features coconut oil as a frying medium instead of vegetable oil, though either can be used. Presenting a plate of hot, crispy fried chicken to a table full of hungry workers is a rite of passage for any southern woman, and this traditional version's buttermilk brine ensures a perfectly juicy final product.*

Serves: 5 (2 pieces per person) | Prep time: 15 minutes | Rest time: 2 hours–overnight
Cook time: 45 minutes | Total time: 1 hour

Ingredients

1 (3-pound) bone-in, skin-on whole chicken, cut into 10 pieces (breasts cut in half)
2 cups buttermilk
2 teaspoons sea salt +
  1 tablespoon sea salt or
  ¾ tablespoon table salt, divided
1 teaspoon black pepper +
  1 teaspoon black pepper divided
4 cups refined coconut oil or vegetable oil, for frying
2 cups all-purpose flour

Instructions

1. Place the chicken pieces in a 9" × 13" baking dish. Pour over the buttermilk, 2 teaspoons sea salt, and 1 teaspoon black pepper. Turn the chicken over in the buttermilk so that the meat and skin are down in the buttermilk. Cover and refrigerate at least 2 hours but overnight is even better.

2. When you're ready to fry, heat a 10-inch cast-iron skillet with oil over medium-high heat to 350°F while you bread the chicken. Add the flour and remaining salt and pepper to a bowl, resealable plastic bag, or paper bag.

3. Make sure the chicken pieces are thoroughly coated in the buttermilk, then place them 2 or 3 at a time in the flour, pressing very firmly to make the flour stick. Set pieces aside for 3 to 5 minutes so that the breading can "set" on the chicken.

4. Heat your oil between 325°F and 350°F. You can test this by dropping the corner of a piece of chicken into the oil. It should sizzle immediately but not smoke. If it just sits there or barely bubbles, your oil is not hot enough; wait about 1 to 2 minutes and try again.

5. When the chicken pieces bubble vigorously, add no more than 4 pieces of chicken to the skillet skin-side down.

Adjust your heat as needed to keep the chicken gently cooking on about medium-low heat, turning each piece every 2 minutes. Turn the pieces up on their ends as needed so that the chicken browns all around.

6. Cook each piece until it reaches 160°F (about 15 to 18 minutes total per batch). Use a meat thermometer to check the temperature if you are unsure.

7. Transfer the cooked chicken to a cooling rack and cook the remaining pieces in batches. Serve warm or cold.

© Rachel Erin Ballard

© Lindsey Kirkland

Mountaintop Scramble

This Mountaintop Scramble is inspired by our family homestead, Kirkland Meadows Farm. Our property sits on the tallest elevation point in Florida. It's called Sugarloaf Mountain and it reaches 312 feet above sea level. To us Floridians, this is huge. It's so nice to go out to the garden and harvest to nourish my ever-growing family of five with this simple recipe. It's savory, southern, and simple. You can throw in just about anything from the garden and it will be delicious. Now, let's get to cooking!

Serves: 4 | Prep time: 10 minutes | Cook time: 20 minutes

Ingredients

4 slices bacon
1 clove garlic, minced
1 sprig rosemary, chopped
¼ cup red onion, chopped
15 baby potatoes, halved
2 cups spinach
Salt and pepper, to taste
15 cherry tomatoes, halved
12 eggs
⅓ cup milk
½ cup Colby-Jack cheese
1 avocado, sliced

Instructions

1. Cook bacon and remove from pan, reserving bacon grease in pan. Chop cooked bacon.

2. Add garlic to pan of bacon grease and cook until fragrant.

3. Add rosemary, onion, and potatoes to pan. Cook on medium heat for approximately 20 minutes until tender and onions are translucent.

4. Remove cooked potato mixture from pan and set aside.

5. Place two handfuls of spinach in the same pan and cook down until just wilted. Add salt and pepper to taste.

6. Add tomatoes to spinach and cook until hot, then set aside.

7. Scramble eggs in a bowl. Add milk, then scramble in a pan. Add more salt and pepper to taste.

8. Layer your plate from bottom to top with scrambled eggs, potatoes, Colby-Jack cheese, spinach-tomato mixture, chopped bacon, and sliced avocado. Serve with warm biscuits and fruit.

Old-Fashioned Sour Cream Donuts

My husband Lorenzo and I started our farm journey once he retired from the US Army after twenty-eight years of service. Our passion for simple country living, cooking, baking, gardening, and taking care of animals is something we wanted to instill in our daughters. We are blessed to be able to run Hidden Gems Farm and to share our farming journey not only with our family but with our community as well. These Old-Fashioned Sour Cream Donuts have become one of our favorite weekend breakfast items to make. If you like funnel cakes, donuts, and churros, this recipe is a must try! Not only are these easy to make, but they taste just as good the next day. (Although we cannot promise that you will have any leftovers.)

Serves: 8 donuts and 8 donut holes | Prep time: 20 minutes | Cook time: 30 minutes

Ingredients

Donuts

2¼ cups cake flour, plus more as needed

1½ teaspoons baking powder

1 teaspoon salt

¼–½ teaspoon nutmeg

2 tablespoons butter at room temperature

½ cup sugar

2 egg yolks

½ cup sour cream

Oil, for frying (I use canola oil)

Glaze

3 cups powdered sugar

1½ teaspoons corn syrup

¼ teaspoon salt

½ teaspoon vanilla extract

⅓ cup hot water (if glaze is too thick, add 1 tablespoon at a time to get a slightly thick consistency)

Instructions

1. For the donuts, in a bowl sift cake flour, baking powder, salt, and nutmeg.

2. Using your stand mixer fitted with a paddle attachment, add butter and sugar. Beat together until mixed well. Add egg yolks and beat until light and thick. Add sour cream to the mixture and mix well.

3. Add dry ingredients to the mixing bowl, a little at a time. Mix on low speed until dough is smooth. The dough will be slightly sticky; if dough is unmanageably sticky, add extra flour 1 tablespoon at a time.

4. Cover with plastic wrap and chill dough until firm, approximately 1 hour.

5. Once chilled, roll out dough on a floured surface to about ½-inch thickness.

6. Use a donut cutter or two different biscuit cutters to cut out as many donuts and donut holes as possible.

7. Heat oil to 325°F. Fry the doughnuts a few at a time. Fry on each side about 2 minutes, being careful not to burn them.

8. For the glaze, in a bowl whisk together glaze ingredients until smooth.

9. Dip donuts into the glaze mixture one at a time. Place on wire cooling rack. Let donuts rest for 10 to 15 minutes or until glaze is set. Enjoy!

© Lorenzo Gibbs

Roasted Cabbage with Dijon-Onion Sauce

Fire Ant Farms is a small family farm located on Johns Island, South Carolina. Our mission is to create a sustainable ecosystem for responsible food production. Through organic growing techniques and regenerative agriculture principles, we are able provide a wide variety and steady supply of fresh produce throughout our year-round growing season. Cabbage is underappreciated, but it is one of our favorite vegetables. Every winter our farmers' market customers ask us what they should do with the cone-shaped Caraflex cabbage, and this recipe never disappoints. It is a simple, inexpensive, and delicious side dish that can be served alongside chicken, beef, or seafood. It is also easily adapted; throw in some caraway and fennel seeds, chili flakes, Parmesan cheese, or heavy cream.

Serving: 6–8 | Prep time: 10–15 minutes | Cook time: 45–50 minutes

Ingredients

Cabbage
2 heads Caraflex cabbage
¼ cup olive oil, divided
Salt and pepper, to taste

Dijon-Onion Sauce
3 tablespoons olive oil
1 medium white or yellow
   onion, chopped
4–5 cloves garlic, minced
½ cup stock
1 tablespoon Dijon mustard
Salt and pepper, to taste

Topping
1 tablespoon olive oil
¼ cup Panko-style bread
   crumbs
⅛ teaspoon dried thyme
⅛ teaspoon garlic powder
Salt and pepper, to taste
Chives, scallions, and
   parsley, to garnish

Instructions

1. Preheat oven to 400°F.

2. For the cabbage, halve cabbage lengthwise through the core. Cut each half into 4 wedges. Place the wedges on a baking sheet. Brush each wedge with olive oil and season with salt and pepper to taste. Flip the wedges and brush the other side with olive oil and season with salt and pepper to taste.

3. Roast in the oven for 15 to 20 minutes. Gently flip the wedges, return to the oven, and roast until wedges are soft and edges are lightly browned, another 10 to 15 minutes.

4. For the sauce, heat olive oil in a medium pan over medium heat. Sauté onions until soft and translucent, 8 to 10 minutes. Add garlic and sauté 1 to 2 minutes. Add stock, reduced until thickened, about 5 to 7 minutes. Reduce heat and add mustard and salt and pepper to taste. Keep warm.

5. For topping, heat olive oil in a small pan over medium heat. In a separate bowl, mix bread crumbs, thyme, garlic powder, and salt and pepper to taste. Add mix to heated pan and stir often until golden brown. Remove from heat.

6. Spoon sauce over cabbage wedges and top with bread crumbs. Garnish with chives, scallions, or parsley. Serve warm.

Green Tomato Relish

Virginia Free Farm is located in the Piedmont of Virginia's beautiful Blue Ridge Mountains in Kents Store, Virginia. We grow heirloom vegetables, mushrooms, seeds, and plants, and raise mixed livestock, all for donation to those in need. This recipe is a traditional way to preserve the end-of-season green tomatoes before the frost blankets the farm. We always use them all up and find our farm customers clamoring for more. It's versatile and can hold its own as a topping on grilled meats or on crackers with a fine artisan cheese.

Serves: 8–10 pints | Prep time: 4 hours | Cook time: 50 minutes

Ingredients

7 pounds green cherry, grape, beefsteak, or Roma tomatoes, quartered (cherry tomatoes can be left whole)

4 large yellow onions, skin and root ends removed and cut into wedges

2 large red onions, skin and root ends removed and cut into wedges

3 large green bell peppers, stems, seeds, and core removed and cut into wedges

2 large red bell peppers, stems, seeds, and core removed and cut into wedges

4 teaspoons canning salt

5 cups apple cider vinegar

4 cups granulated sugar

2 tablespoons celery seed

4 teaspoons mustard seed

Instructions

1. In a food processor, process tomatoes, onions, and peppers in batches until finely chopped.

2. Combine vegetables in a large bowl and stir in canning salt. Divide the vegetable mixture between two large strainers and place the strainers over a deep bowl to strain.

3. Let the vegetables sit for about 3 hours to strain. If you'd like, use the back of a large spoon or the back of a smaller mesh strainer with handle, press on the vegetables, and encourage them to strain more quickly.

4. Discard the liquid that the vegetables released during the straining process. Pour strained vegetables into a large 12-quart stockpot. Add in vinegar, sugar, celery seed, and mustard seed, then stir to combine.

5. Bring mixture to a boil. Reduce heat to a moderate simmer and cook uncovered for 30 to 35 minutes, stirring frequently. The mixture should be thickened with most of the liquid simmered off.

6. While the relish mixture is simmering, prepare a large pot of water or a water-bath canner. Heat pint jars in simmering water until ready to use. Wash lids and bands, as well as a ladle and funnel with warm, soapy water. Set aside until ready to use.

7. Once the relish mixture has simmered and thickened, carefully ladle the hot relish into the prepared pint jars,

© Amy Rose Foll

leaving ½-inch head space. Remove air bubbles and wipe rims clean. Place lids on the jars; screw on bands until finger tight.

8. Place jars in a large pot of water or a water-bath canner with simmering water, making sure that the tops of the jars are covered with water. Bring to a boil and process for 15 minutes. Carefully remove jars and cool on a rack, checking to make sure that the jars are sealed once cool.

Founder Patti Johnson-Long
© Salina Long

Founder's Story

Creative maker, baker, and lover of all things farm, my childhood was spent hopping family farms in North Dakota every summer. Past our parents' sudden death, my four sisters, brother, and German grandparents felt happily distracted there and celebrated. We attended farm weddings, anniversaries, and family reunions full of culturally specific farm food, polka dancing, and the freedom to be ourselves. Moving on bravely to travel the world, get my college degree, and raise a family of my own with my childhood sweetheart, I eventually embraced my heart's desire.

Convincing my "city slicker" husband to build me a chicken coop and fill it with chickens so that "the kids could learn the meaning of responsibility and hard work" was the easy part. Insisting that we then build a barn, get goats, pigs, ducks, turkeys, and *more* chickens was a little bit harder. (When you wrangle your first goat together to trim hooves, you know it's official.) Our teamwork, passion for nutritious food, and the realization that farm animals are completely entertaining, led us to create FarmMade.

Acknowledgments

Embarking on this cookbook was a life's dream of mine and would never have been possible without the amazing and continued support of my mother- and father-in-law, Delores and Tom Long. They provided the resources I needed to finish my college degree, along with a beautiful homestead "on the hill" from which to launch the FarmMade business. They then held their breath with a certain amount of finesse and understanding, gifting me the confidence to accomplish what I set out to do. You both are *amazing* people and I thank you from the bottom of my heart.

I am eternally grateful to my daughter, Salina. From researching fabulous farms to include, to proofreading recipes, and the biggest job of all, helping me edit the final manuscript, she was as important to this book getting done as I was. Thank you for being my best friend, best daughter, and best partner ever!

My dear, sweet husband, Rex, you have been my cheerleader and never-ending support system from the beginning. Your love keeps me steady and always reaching for stars that seem impossible to grab. I have asked for so much and you have given me all of it. You have a heart of gold and work hands of steel. This blessed farm life would be impossible without you.

I am grateful every day that God granted me a son like you, Robert. You bring the magic! A magic that lights up your face and seems to glow in the dark. Your exuberance is contagious. Your spark is undeniable. Your love for chickens and all the funny things they do truly brightens my day and brings me so much joy. The four fluffy butt Orpingtons you named "Tima" will go down in history as our favorite farm mascots.

A very special thanks to all the farmers who took the time out of their busy "sun-up to sundown" farm lives to share a traditional family recipe. Your dedication to providing good food and great service to your community inspires me daily. As a small child, I felt like the farm was my very own playground. Your down-home way of making me feel celebrated as a child has enriched my whole life and I owe you a humble "thank you" for persevering against all odds to do what you do. I adore every single one of you and wish you the utmost success.

Conversion Charts

METRIC AND IMPERIAL CONVERSIONS

(These conversions are rounded for convenience)

Ingredient	Cups/Tablespoons/Teaspoons	Ounces	Grams/Milliliters
Butter	1 cup/ 16 tablespoons/ 2 sticks	8 ounces	230 grams
Cheese, shredded	1 cup	4 ounces	110 grams
Cream cheese	1 tablespoon	0.5 ounce	14.5 grams
Cornstarch	1 tablespoon	0.3 ounce	8 grams
Flour, all-purpose	1 cup/1 tablespoon	4.5 ounces/0.3 ounce	125 grams/8 grams
Flour, whole wheat	1 cup	4 ounces	120 grams
Fruit, dried	1 cup	4 ounces	120 grams
Fruits or veggies, chopped	1 cup	5 to 7 ounces	145 to 200 grams
Fruits or veggies, pureed	1 cup	8.5 ounces	245 grams
Honey, maple syrup, or corn syrup	1 tablespoon	0.75 ounce	20 grams
Liquids: cream, milk, water, or juice	1 cup	8 fluid ounces	240 milliliters
Oats	1 cup	5.5 ounces	150 grams
Salt	1 teaspoon	0.2 ounce	6 grams
Spices: cinnamon, cloves, ginger, or nutmeg (ground)	1 teaspoon	0.2 ounce	5 milliliters
Sugar, brown, firmly packed	1 cup	7 ounces	200 grams
Sugar, white	1 cup/1 tablespoon	7 ounces/0.5 ounce	200 grams/12.5 grams
Vanilla extract	1 teaspoon	0.2 ounce	4 grams

OVEN TEMPERATURES

Fahrenheit	Celsius	Gas Mark
225°	110°	¼
250°	120°	½
275°	140°	1
300°	150°	2
325°	160°	3
350°	180°	4
375°	190°	5
400°	200°	6
425°	220°	7
450°	230°	8

Index

Grain-Free Italian Stuffed Peppers, 132–133